The New York Times

WILL SHORTZ PRESENTS SUNDAY
KENKEN™

300 CHALLENGING PUZZLES
THAT MAKE YOU SMARTER

TETSUYA MIYAMOTO

INTRODUCTION BY
WILL SHORTZ

ST. MARTIN'S GRIFFIN
NEW YORK

www.stmartins.com

ISBN 978-0-312-62179-7

First Edition: October 2009

10 9 8 7 6 5 4 3 2 1

Introduction

If you consider all the world's greatest puzzle varieties, the ones that have inspired crazes over the years—crosswords, jigsaw puzzles, tangrams, sudoku, etc.—they have several properties in common. They . . .

- Are simple to learn
- Have great depth
- Are variable in difficulty, from easy to hard
- Are mentally soothing and pleasing
- Have some unique feature that makes them different from everything else and instantly addictive

By these standards, a new puzzle called KenKen, the subject of the book you're holding, has the potential to become one of the world's greats.

KenKen is Japanese for "square wisdom" or "cleverness squared." The rules are simple: Fill the grid with digits so as not to repeat a digit in any row or column (as in sudoku) and so the digits within each heavily outlined group of boxes combine to make the arithmetic result indicated.

The simplest KenKen puzzles start with 3×3 boxes and use only addition. Harder examples have larger grids and more arithmetic operations.

KenKen was invented in 2003 by Tetsuya Miyamoto, a Japanese math instructor, as a means to help his students learn arithmetic and develop logical thinking. Tetsuya's education method is unusual. Put simply, he doesn't teach.

His philosophy is to make the tools of learning available to students and then let them progress on their own.

Tetsuya's most popular learning tool has been KenKen, which his students spend hours doing and find more engaging than TV and video games.

It's true that KenKen has great capacity for educating and building the mind. But first and foremost it's a puzzle to be enjoyed. It is to numbers what the crossword puzzle is to words.

So turn the page and begin. . . .

—Will Shortz

How to Solve KenKen

KenKen is a logic puzzle with simple rules:

- Fill the grid with digits so as not to repeat a digit in any row or column.
- Digits within each heavily outlined group of squares, called a cage, must combine to make the arithmetic result indicated.
- A 3×3–square puzzle will use the digits from 1 to 3, a 4×4–square puzzle will use the digits from 1 to 4, etc.

Solving a KenKen puzzle involves pure logic and mathematics. No guesswork is needed. Every puzzle has a unique solution.

In this volume of KenKen, the puzzles use all four arithmetic operations—addition, subtraction, multiplication, and division—in the following manner:

- In a cage marked with a plus sign, the given number will be the sum of the digits you enter in the squares.
- In a cage marked with a minus sign, the given number will be the difference between the digits you enter in the squares (the lower digit subtracted from the higher one).

Take the 5×5–square example on this page.

48×		3+		4−
	8+	10×	4+	
3−				2÷
	4+		4	
7+			15×	

To start, fill in any digits in 1×1 sections—in this puzzle, the 4 in the fourth row. These are literally no-brainers.

Next, look for sections whose given numbers are either high or low, or that involve distinctive combinations of digits, since these are often the easiest to solve. For example, the L-shaped group in the upper left has a product of 48. The only combination of three digits from 1 to 5 that multiplies to 48 is 3, 4, and 4. Since the two 4s can't appear in the same row or column, they must appear at the ends of the L. The 3 goes between them.

Now look at the pair of squares in the first row with a sum of 3. The only two digits that add up to 3 are 1 and 2. We don't know their order yet, but this information can still be useful.

Sometimes, the next step in solving a KenKen puzzle is to ignore the given numbers and use sudoku-like logic to avoid repeating a digit in a row or column. For example, now that 1, 2, 3, and 4 have been used or are slated for use in the first row, the remaining square (at the end of the row) must be a 5. Then the digit below the 5 must be a 1 for this pair of squares to have a difference of 4.

Next, consider the pair of squares in the third column with a product of 10. The only two digits from 1 to 5 that have a product of 10 are 2 and 5. We

48× 3	4	3+ 1	2	4− 5
4	8+ 5	10× 2	4+ 3	1
3− 2	3	5	1	2÷ 4
5	4+ 1	3	4 4	2
7+ 1	2	4	15× 5	3

don't know their order yet. However, the digit in the square above them, which we previously identified as either a 1 or a 2, must be 1, so as not to repeat a 2 in this column. The 2 that accompanies the 1 goes to its right.

Continuing in this way, using these and other techniques left for you to discover, you can work your way around the grid, filling in the rest of the squares. The complete solution is shown above.

Additional Tips
- In advanced KenKen puzzles, as you've seen, cages can have more than two squares. It's okay for a cage to repeat a digit—as long as the digit is not repeated in a row or column.
- Cages with more than two squares will always involve addition or multiplication. Subtraction and division occur only in cages with exactly two squares.
- Remember, in doing KenKen, you never have to guess. Every puzzle can be solved by using step-by-step logic. Keep going, and soon you'll be a KenKen master!

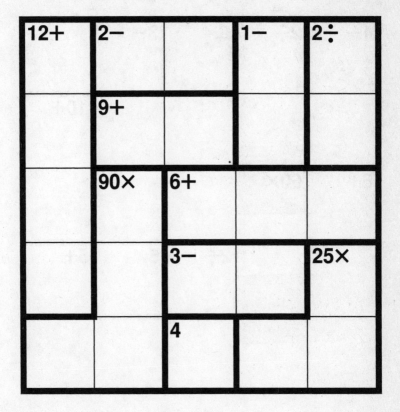

Moderate +/−/×/÷

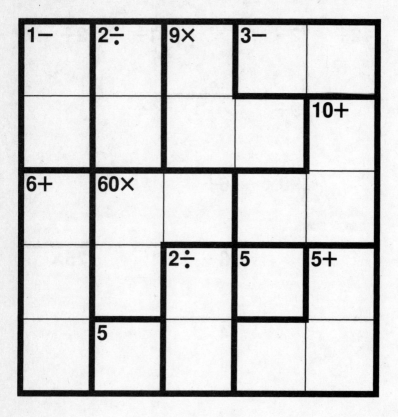

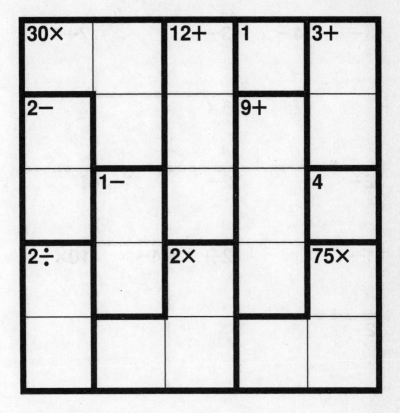

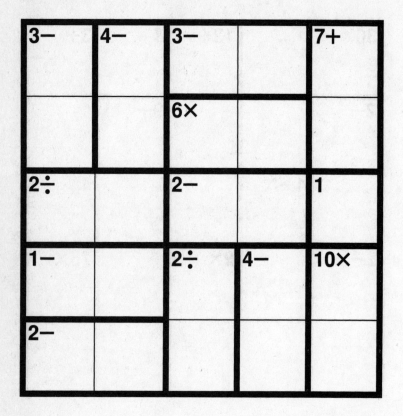

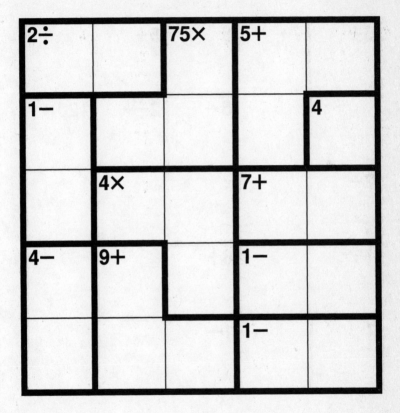

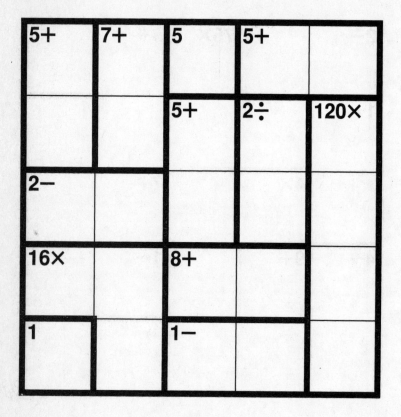

5+	7+	5	5+	
120X		5+	2÷	120X
2−				
16X		8+		
1		1−		

Moderate +/−/×/÷

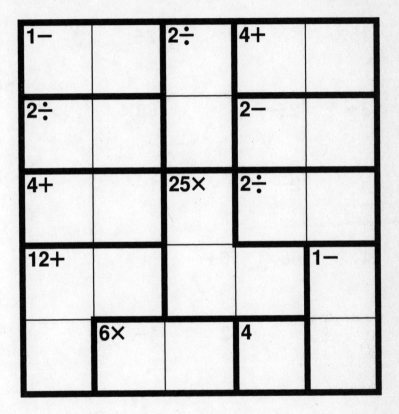

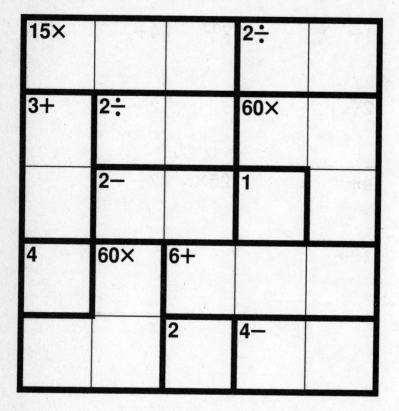

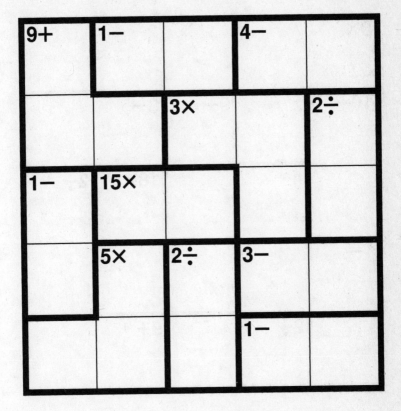

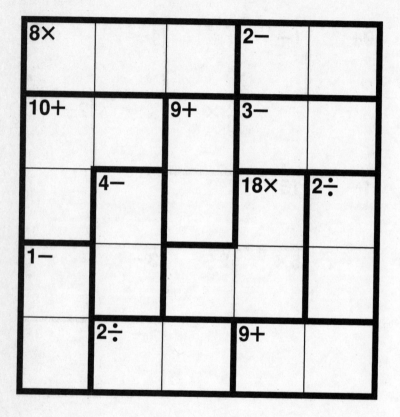

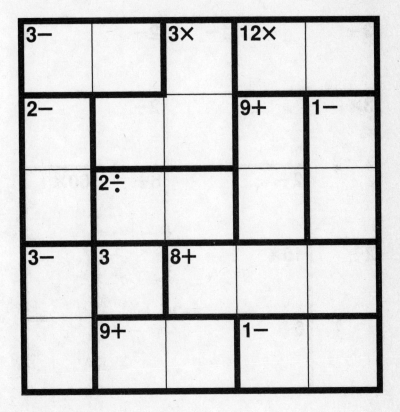

Moderate +/−/×/÷

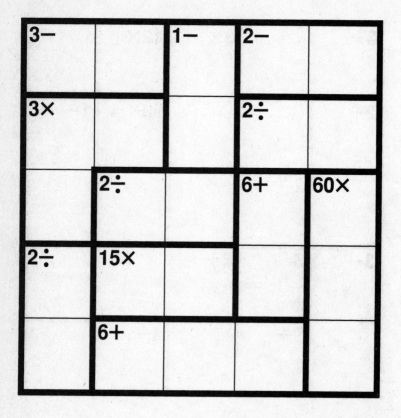

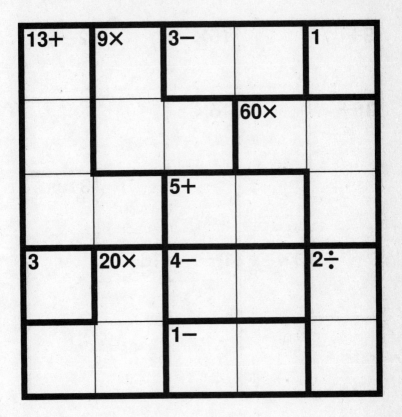

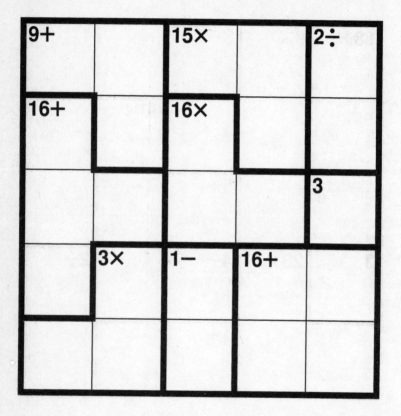

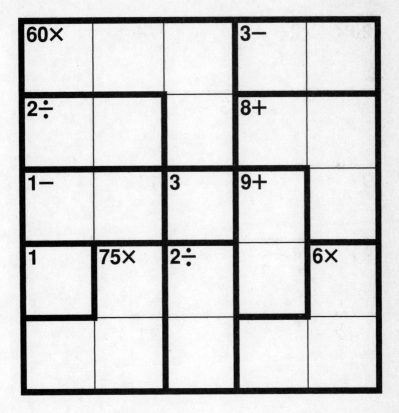

60×			3−	
2÷			8+	
1−		3	9+	
1	75×	2÷		6×

Moderate +/−/×/÷

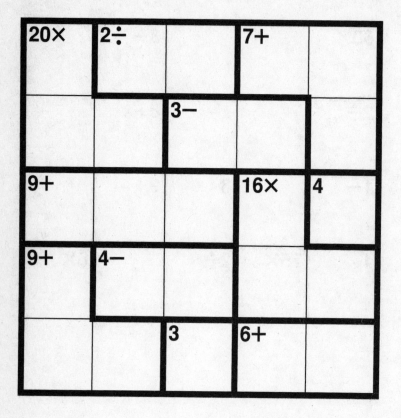

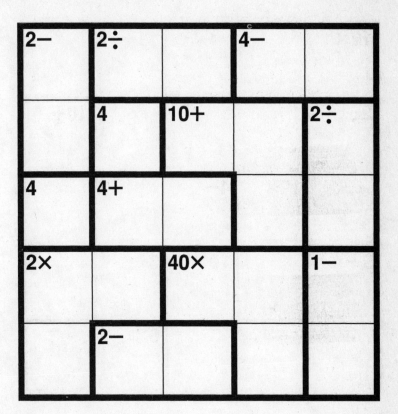

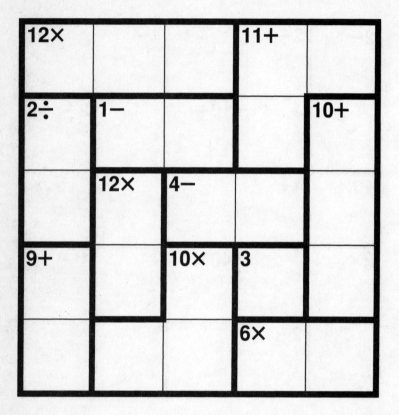

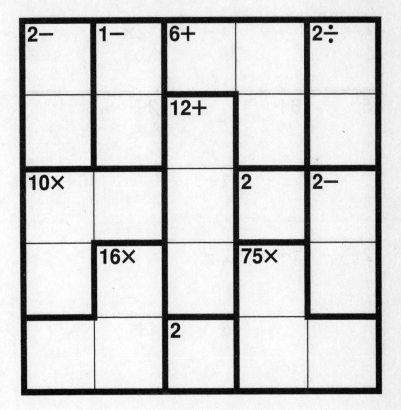

Moderate +/−/×/÷

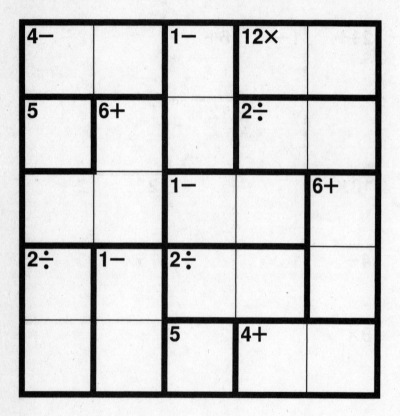

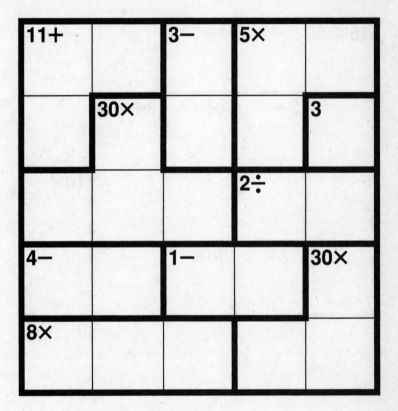

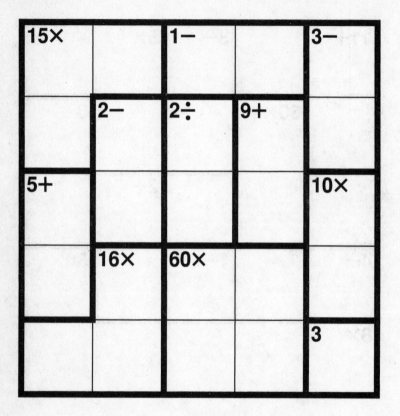

Moderate +/−/×/÷

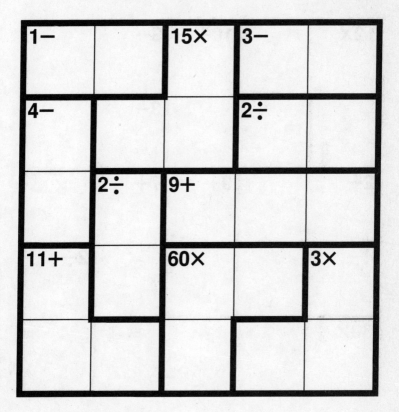

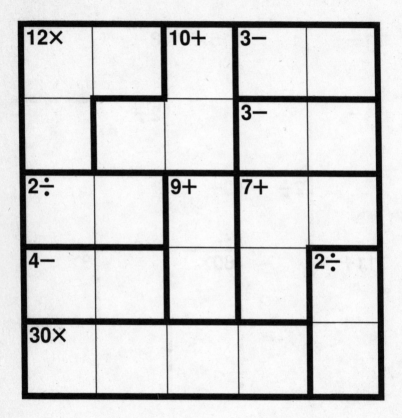

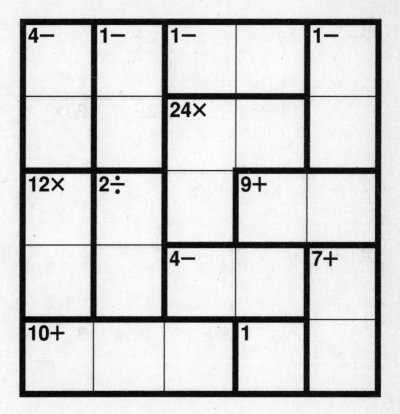

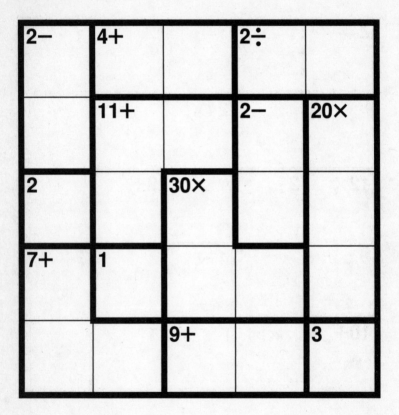

Moderate +/−/×/÷

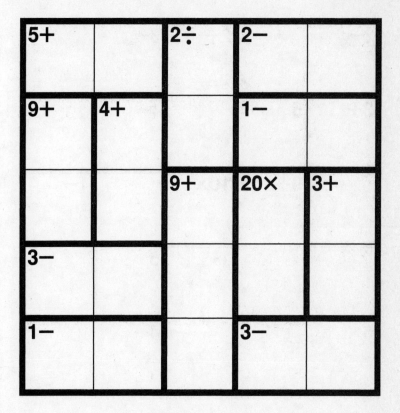

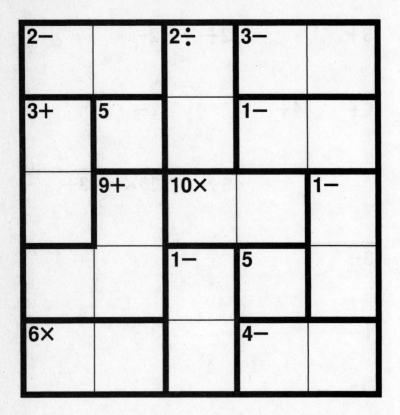

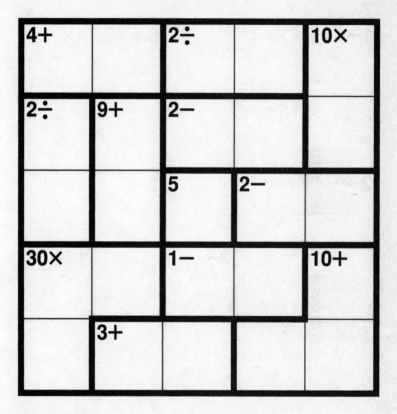

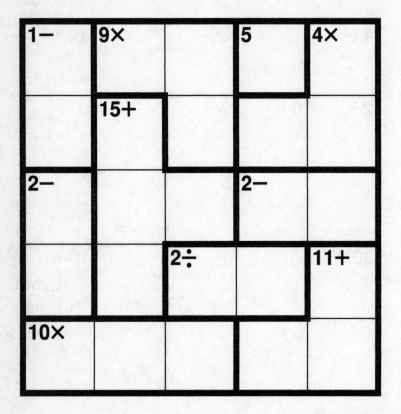

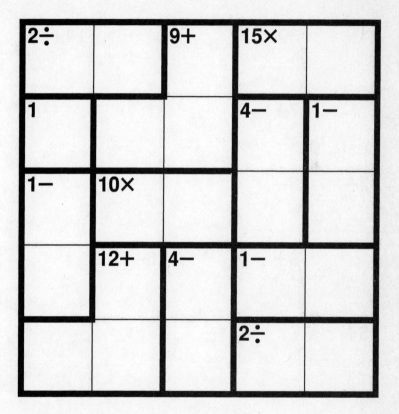

2÷		9+	15×	
1			4−	1−
1−	10×			
	12+	4−	1−	
			2÷	

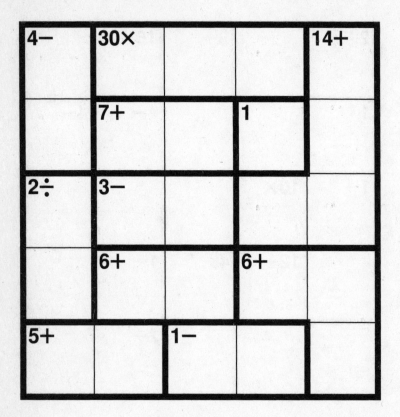

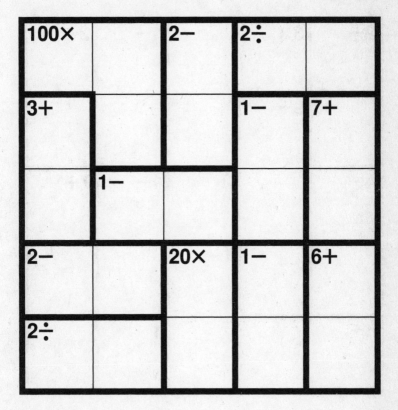

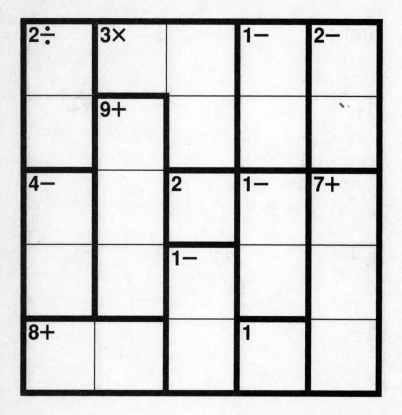

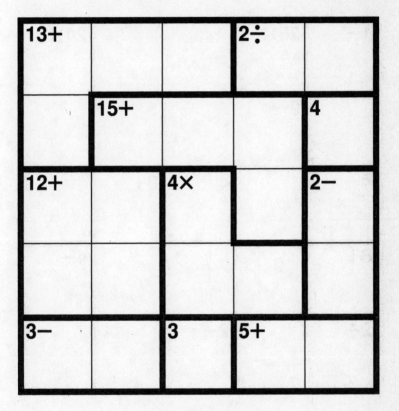

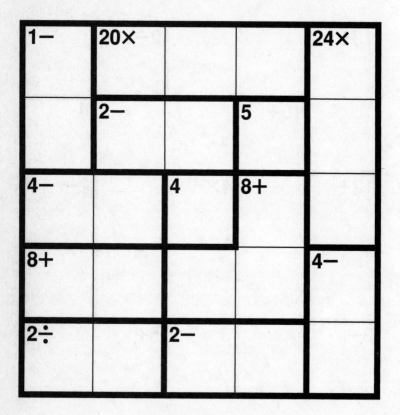

Moderate +/−/×/÷

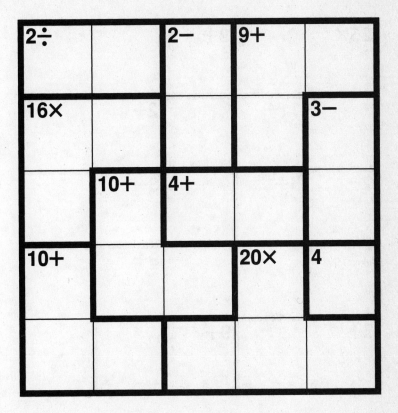

2÷		2−	9+	
16×				3−
	10+	4+		
10+			20×	4

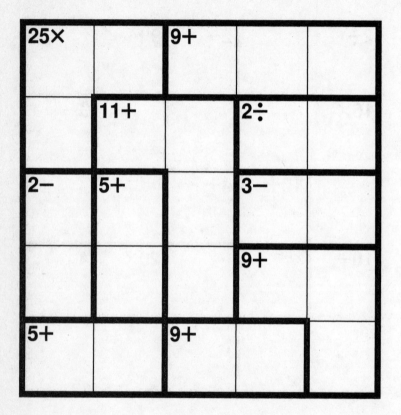

Moderate +/−/×/÷

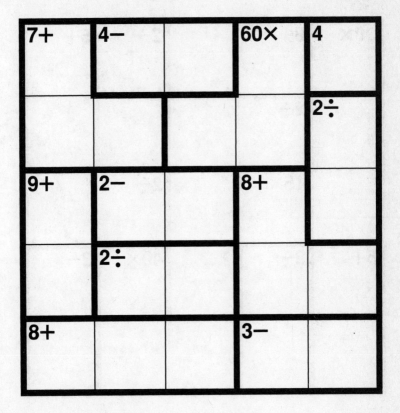

7+	4−		60×	4
				2÷
9+	2−		8+	
	2÷			
8+			3−	

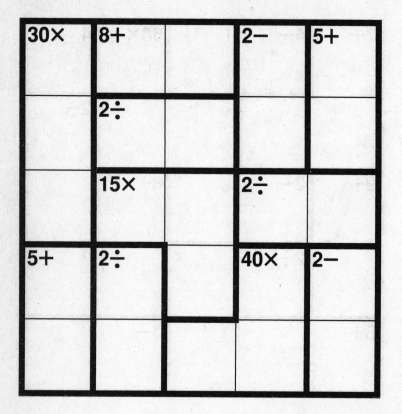

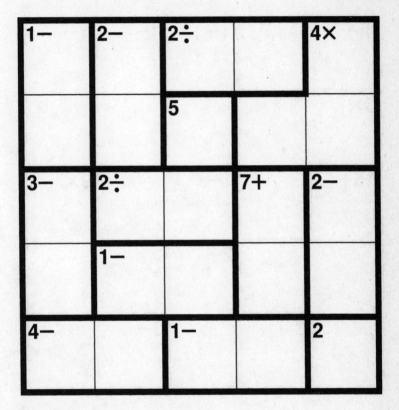

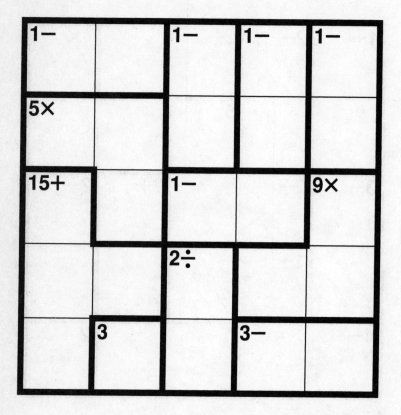

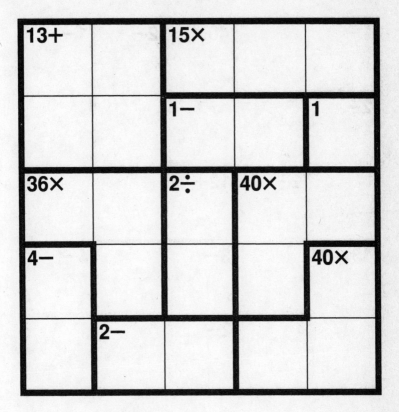

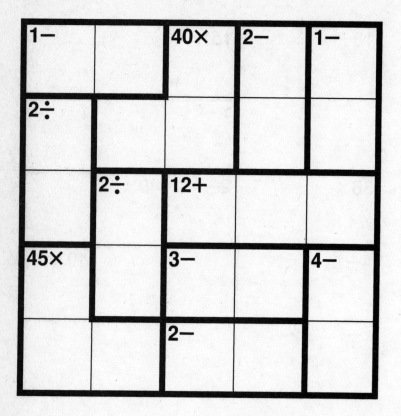

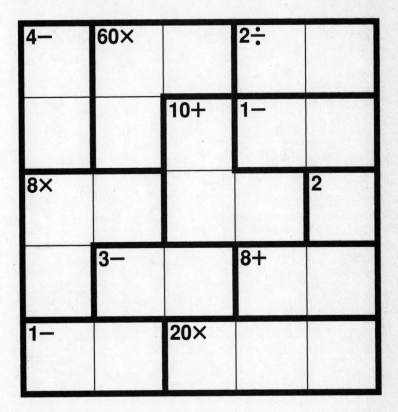

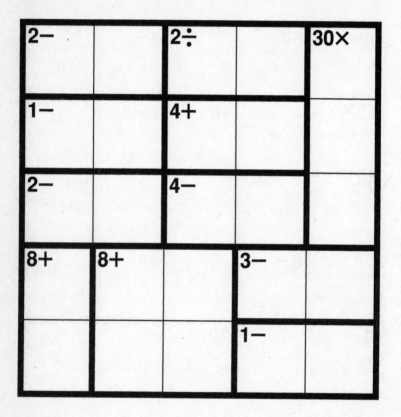

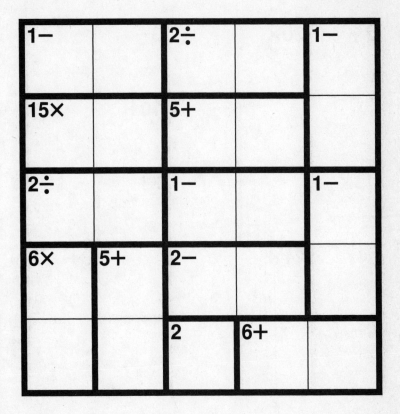

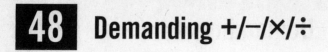

48 Demanding +/−/×/÷

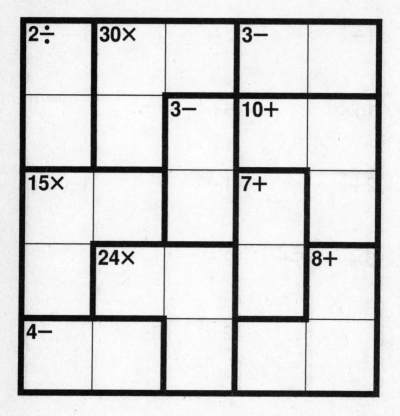

2÷	30×		3−	
		3−	10+	
15×			7+	
	24×			8+
4−				

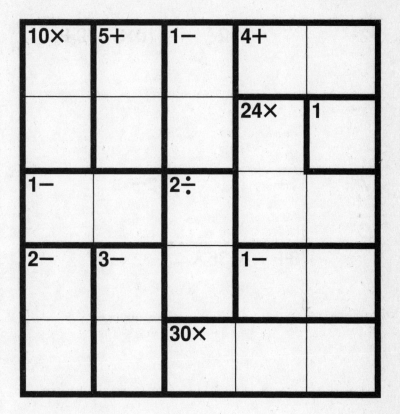

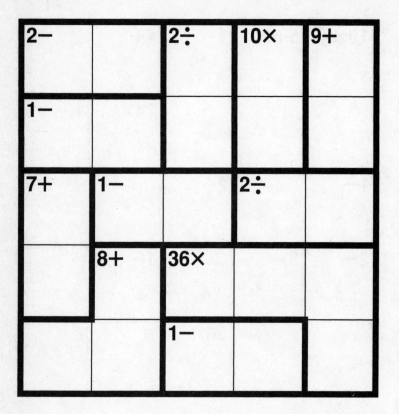

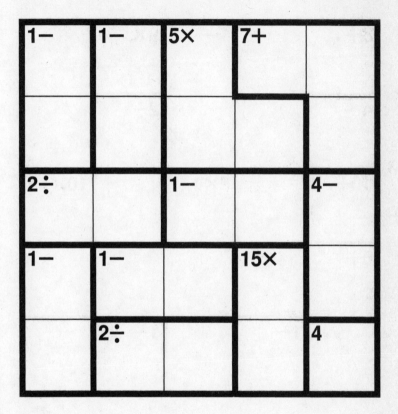

52 Demanding +/−/×/÷

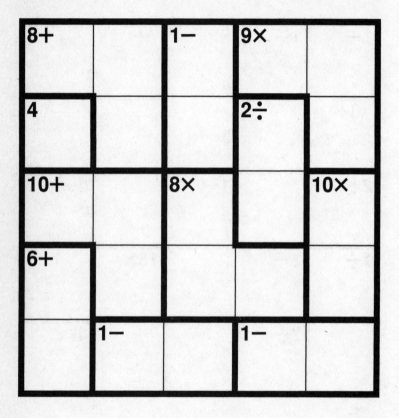

Demanding +/−/×/÷

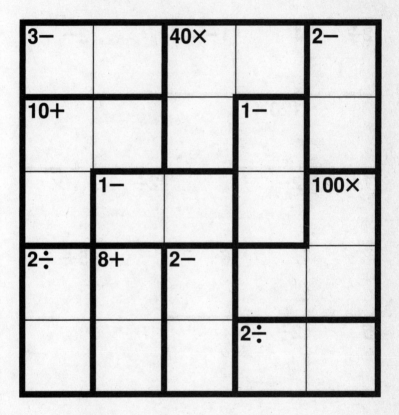

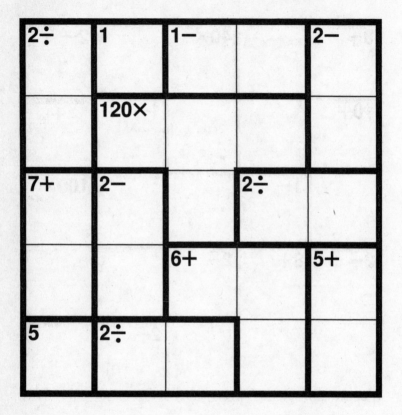

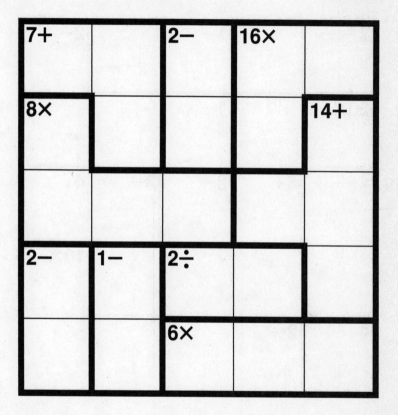

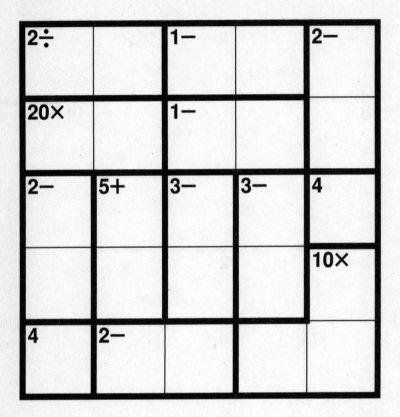

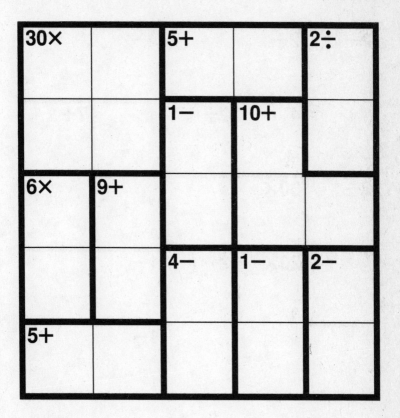

58 Demanding +/−/×/÷

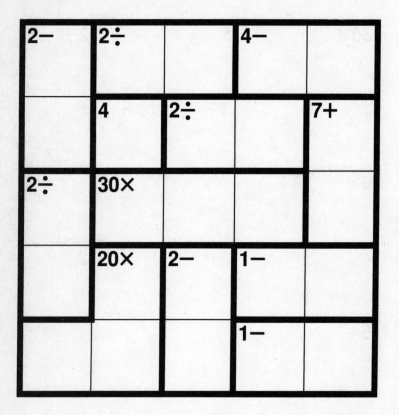

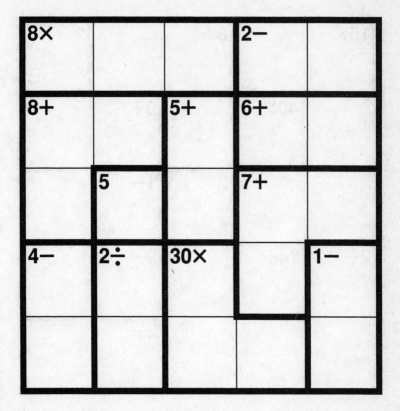

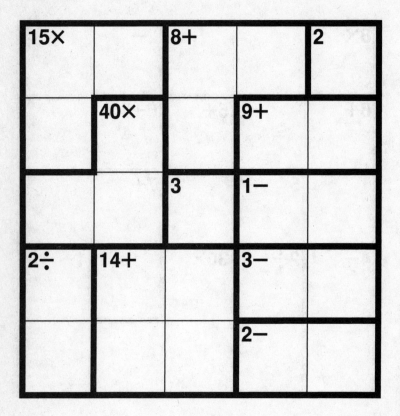

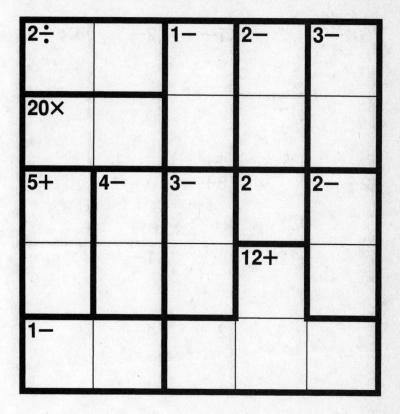

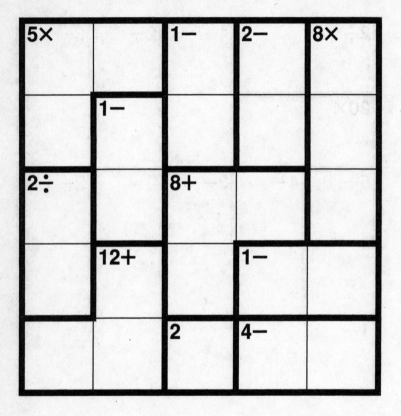

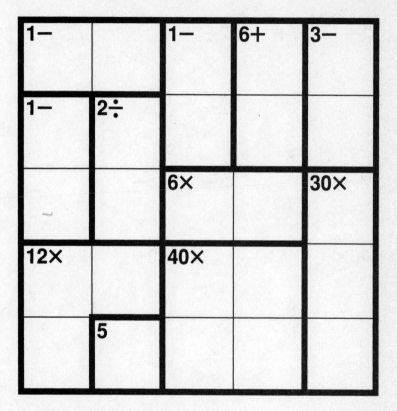

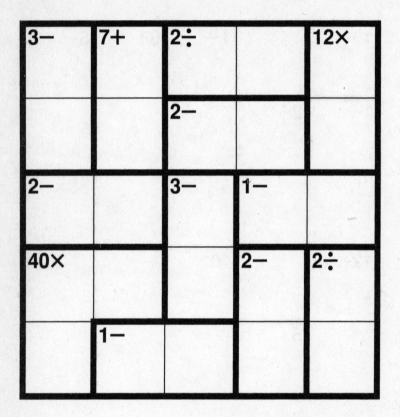

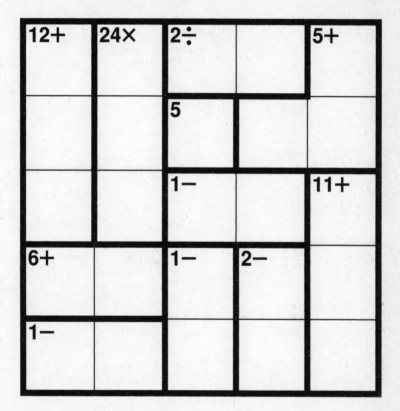

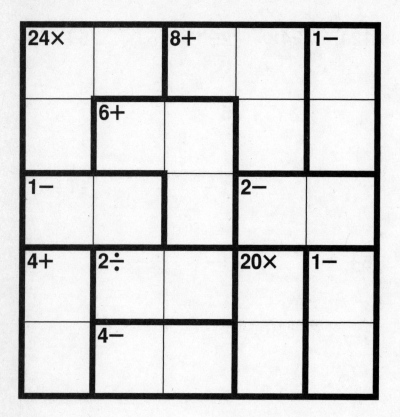

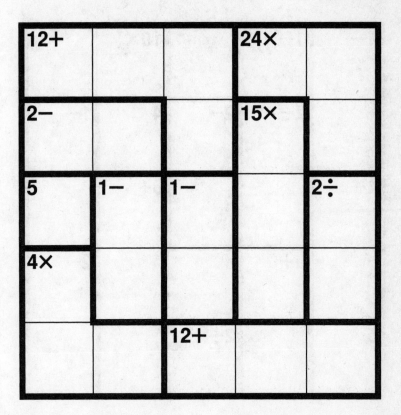

Demanding +/−/×/÷

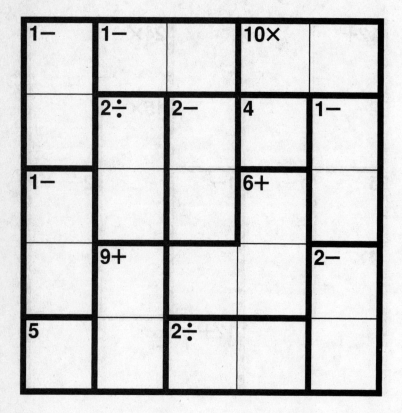

Demanding +/−/×/÷

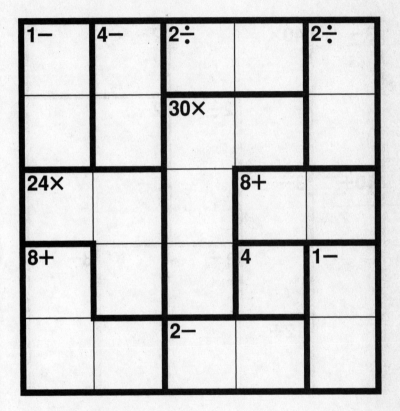

Demanding +/−/×/÷

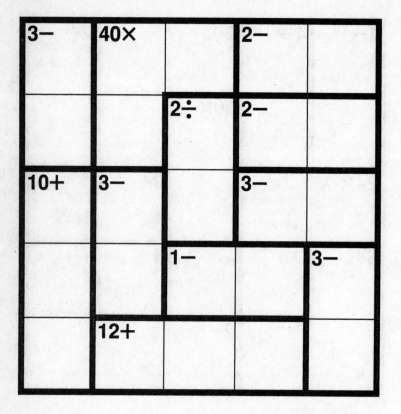

3−	40×		2−	
		2÷	2−	
10+	3−		3−	
		1−		3−
	12+			

Demanding +/−/×/÷   71

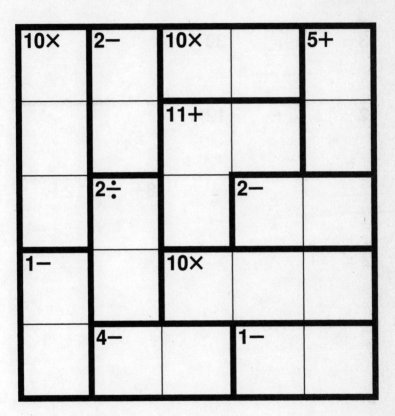

Demanding +/−/×/÷

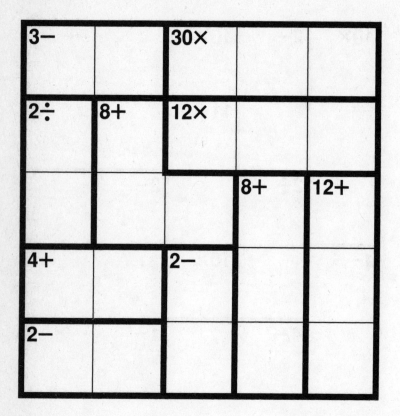

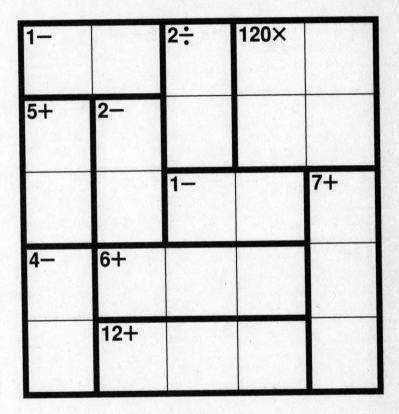

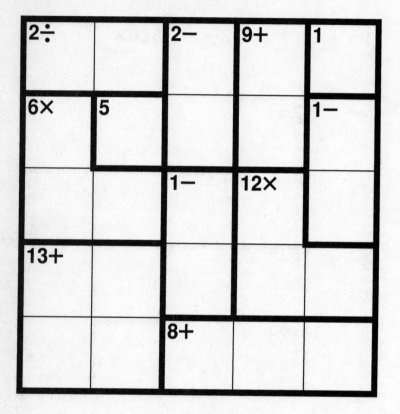

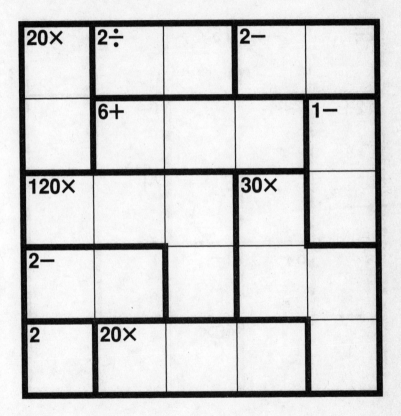

20×	2÷		2−	
120×	6+			1−
120×			30×	
2−				
2	20×			

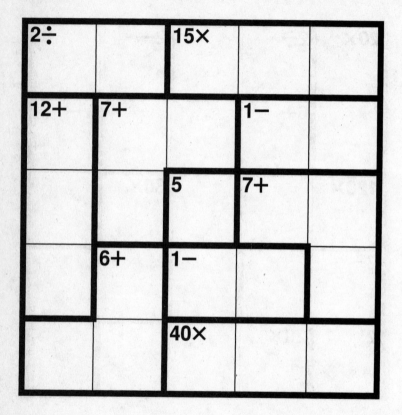

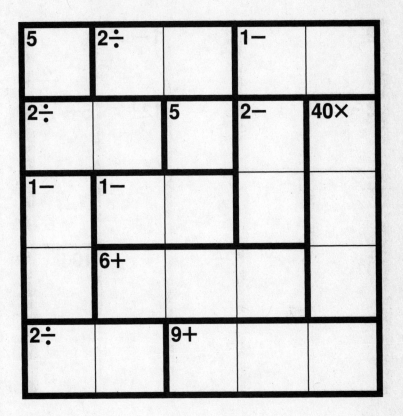

78 Demanding +/−/×/÷

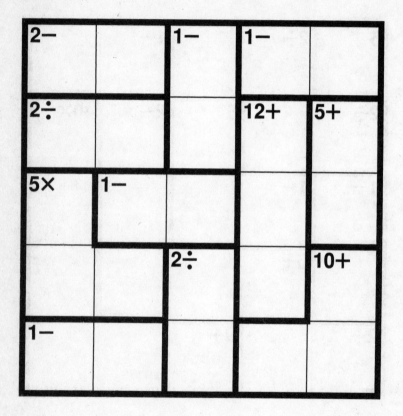

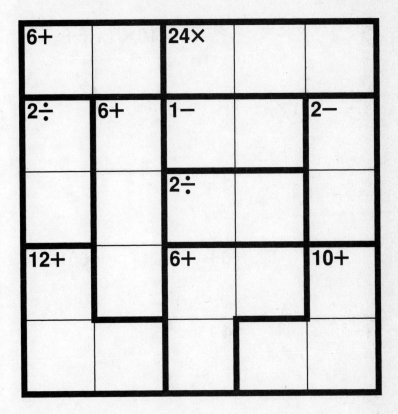

Demanding +/−/×/÷

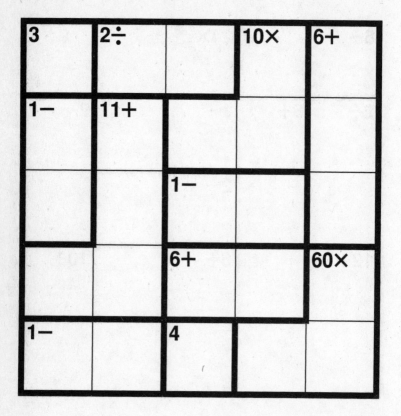

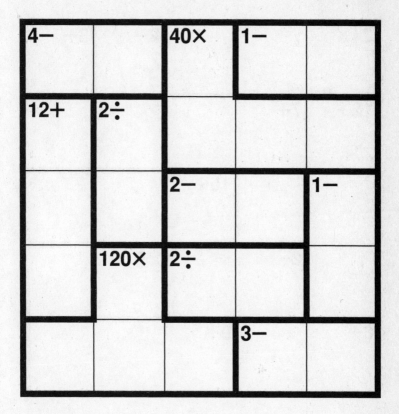

82 Demanding +/−/×/÷

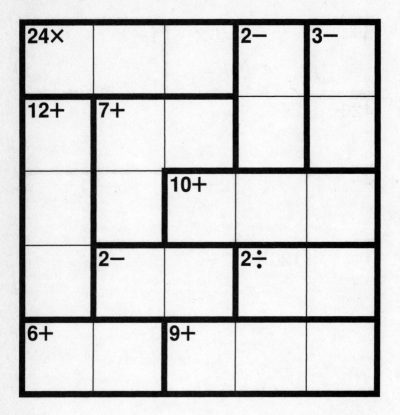

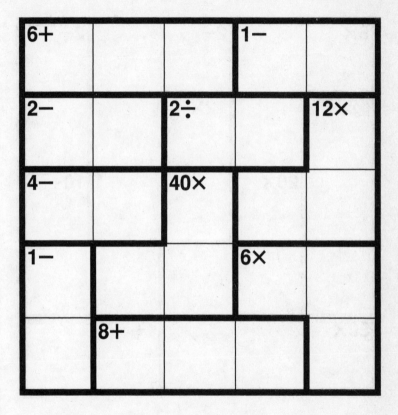

Demanding +/−/×/÷

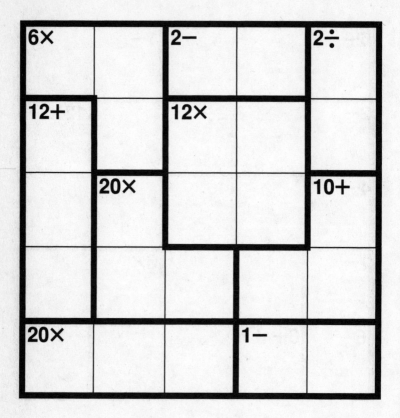

Demanding +/−/×/÷

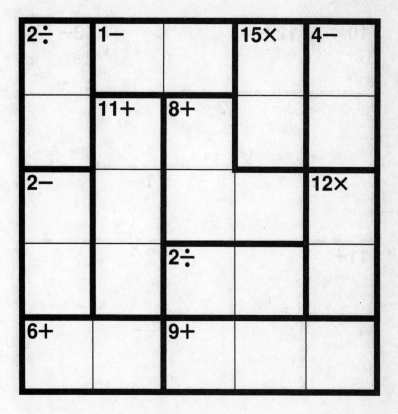

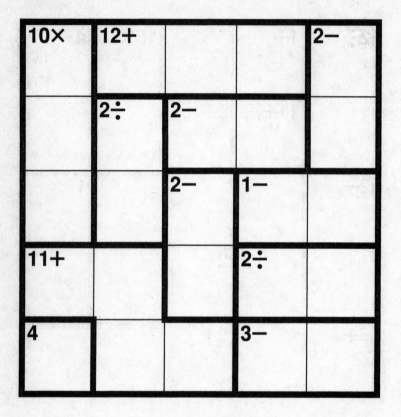

Very Challenging +/−/×/÷

40×	60×			8+
		2÷		
12×	4−		2	
		2−	1−	
1−			1−	

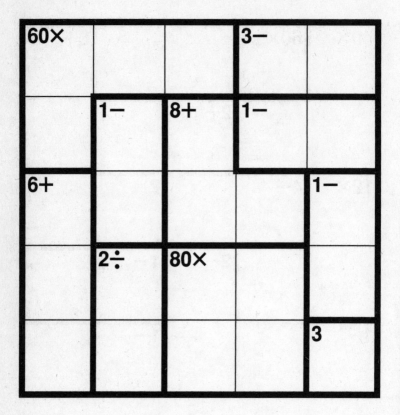

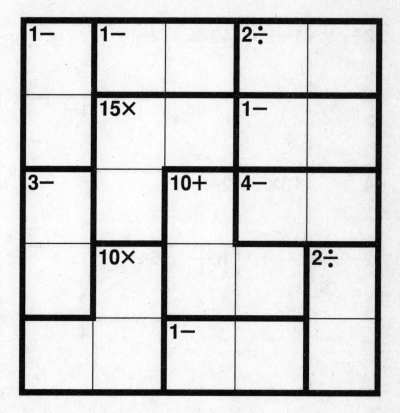

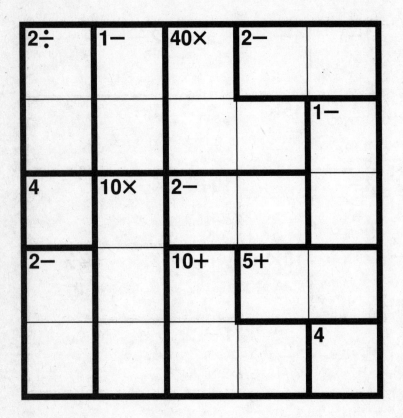

Very Challenging +/−/×/÷

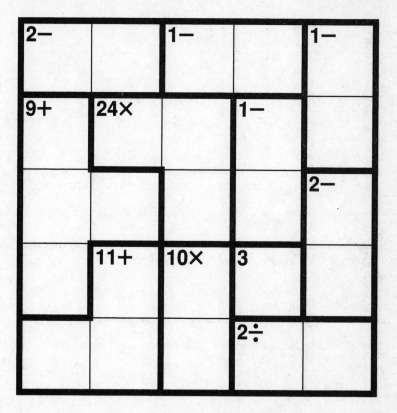

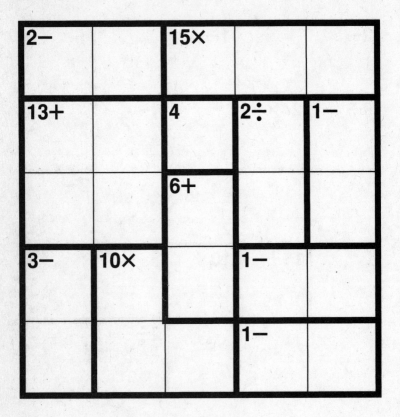

Very Challenging +/−/×/÷

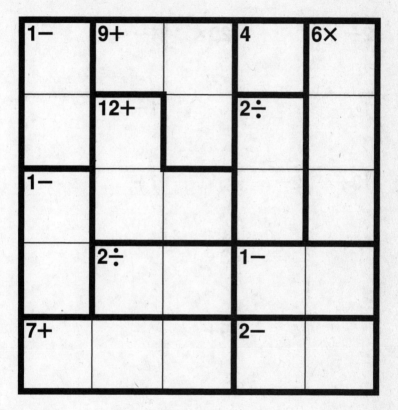

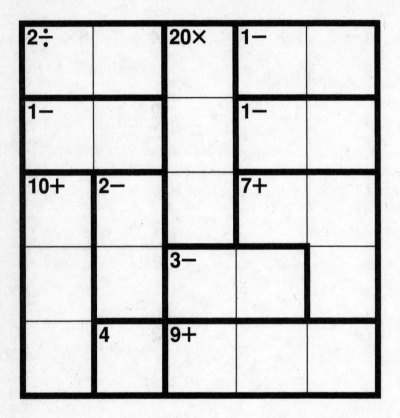

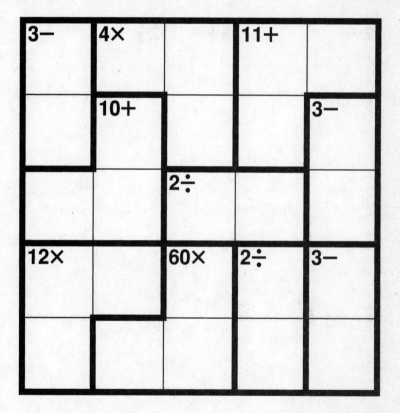

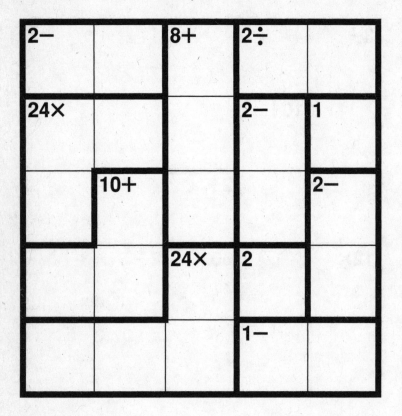

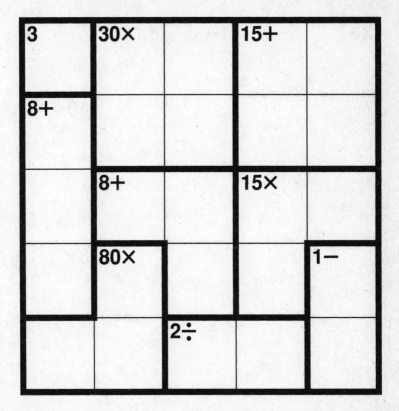

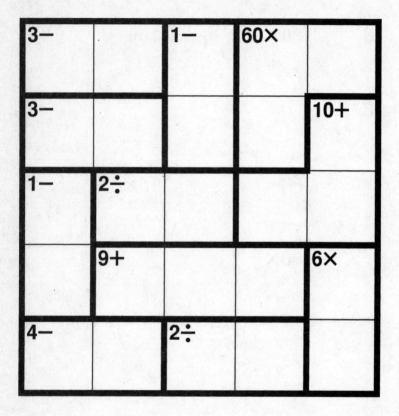

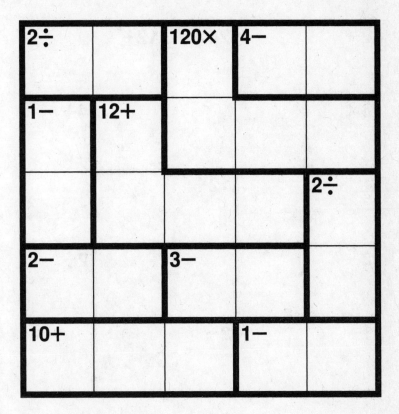

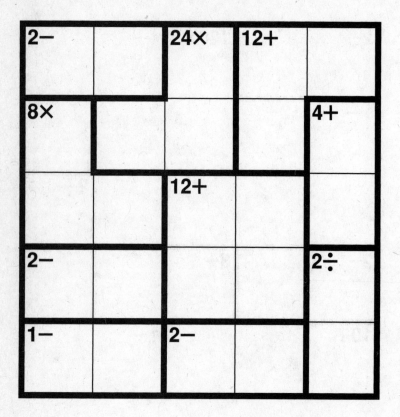

Very Challenging +/−/×/÷

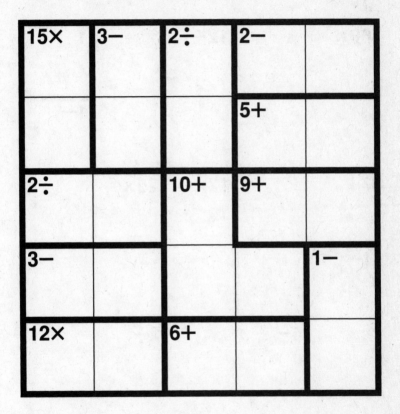

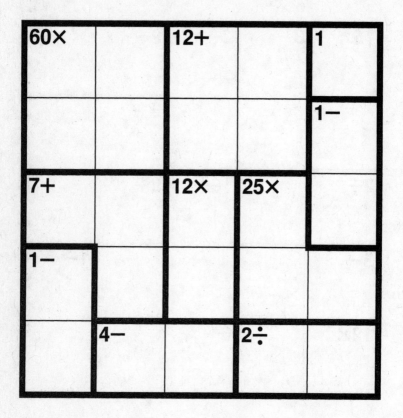

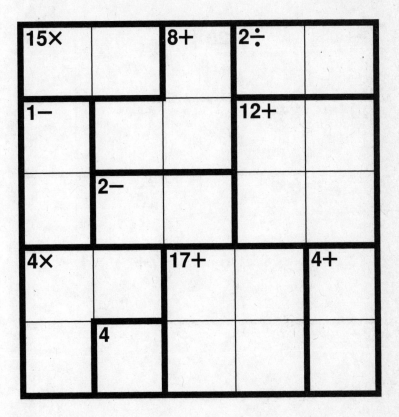

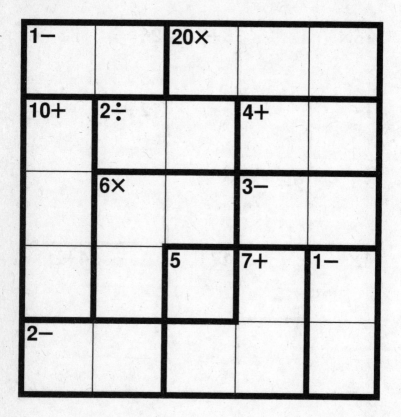

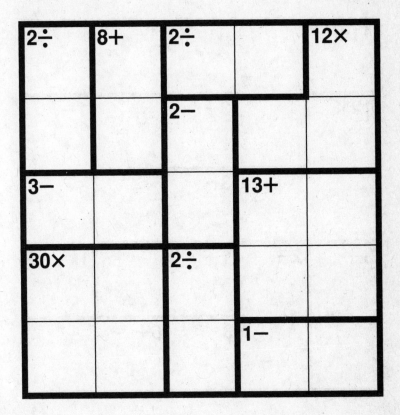

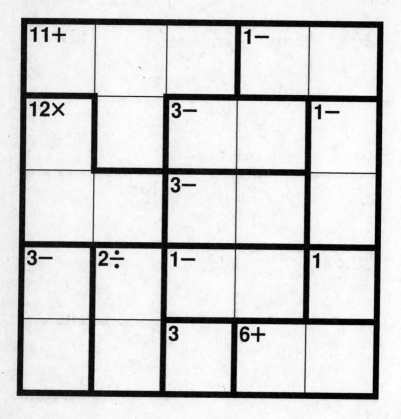

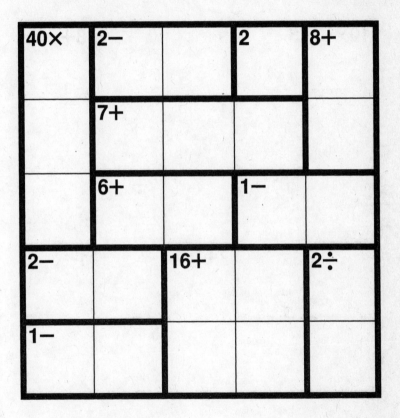

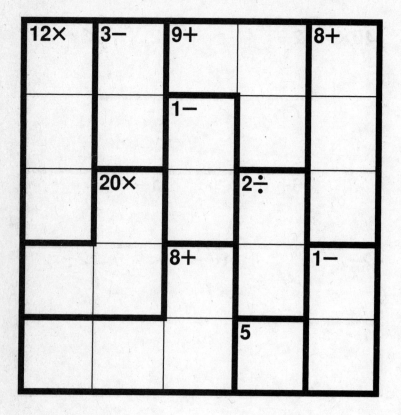

Very Challenging +/−/×/÷

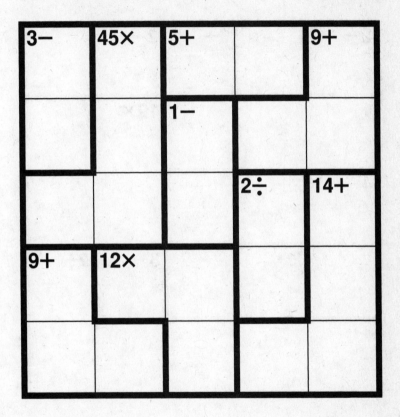

110 Very Challenging +/−/×/÷

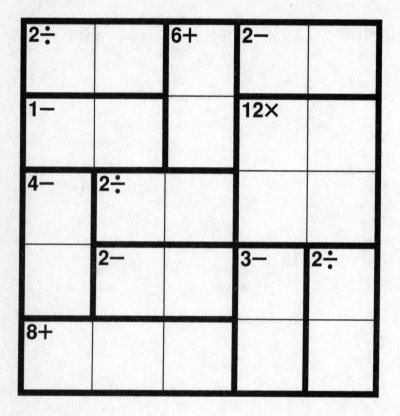

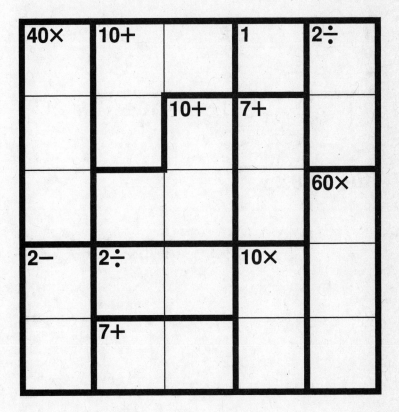

112 Very Challenging +/−/×/÷

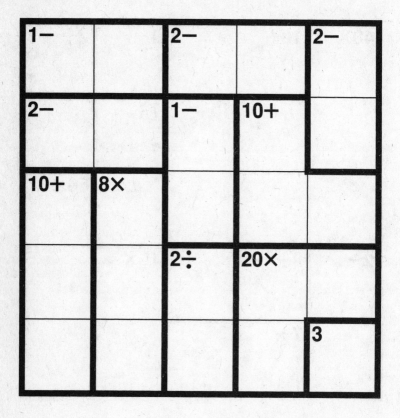

Very Challenging +/−/×/÷ 113

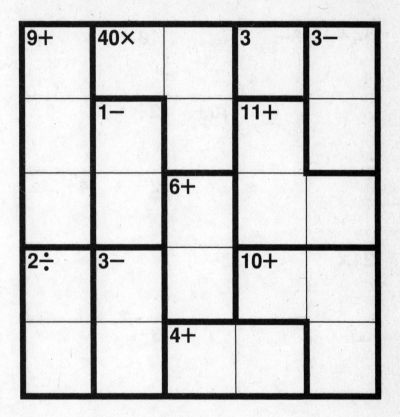

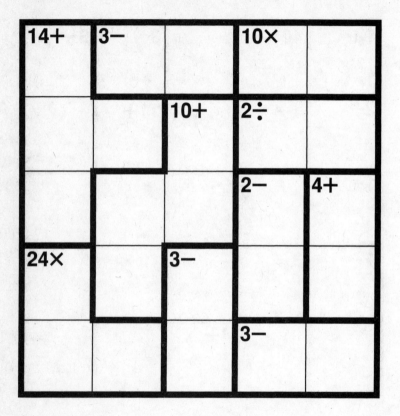

Very Challenging +/−/×/÷ 115

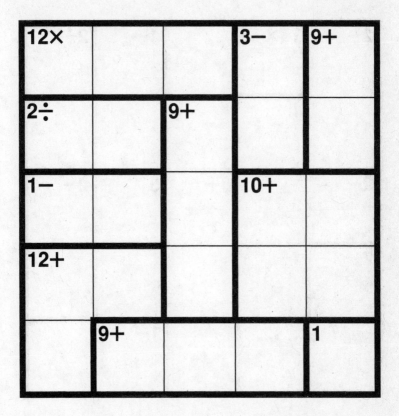

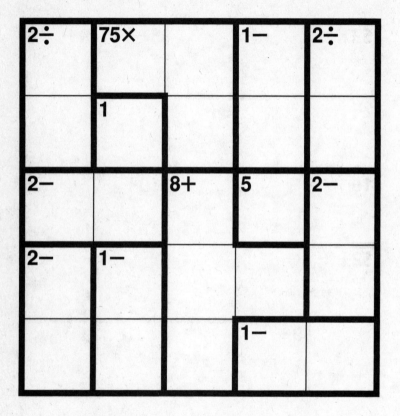

Very Challenging +/−/×/÷

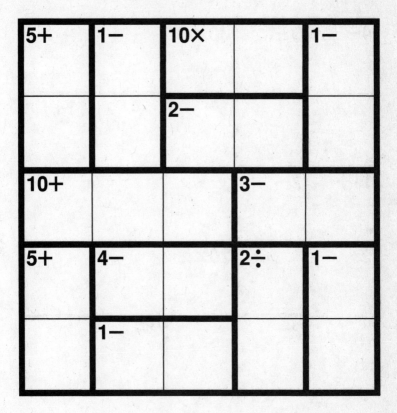

5+	1−	10×		1−
		2−		
10+			3−	
5+	4−		2÷	1−
	1−			

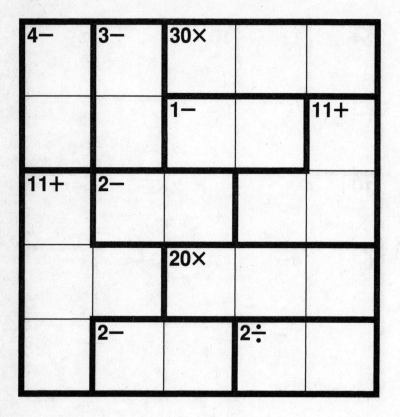

Very Challenging +/−/×/÷

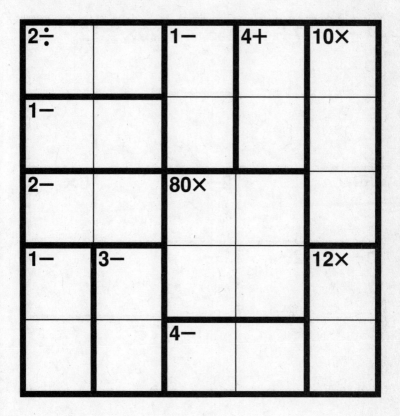

120 Very Challenging +/−/×/÷

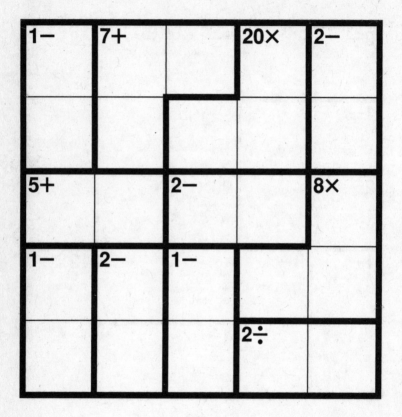

Very Challenging +/−/×/÷ 121

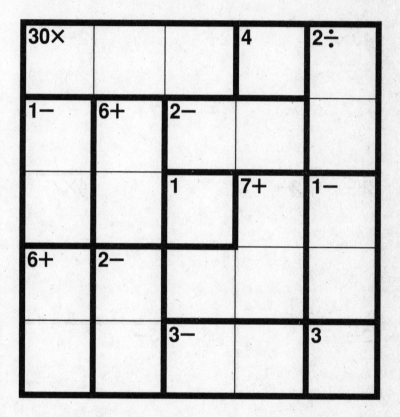

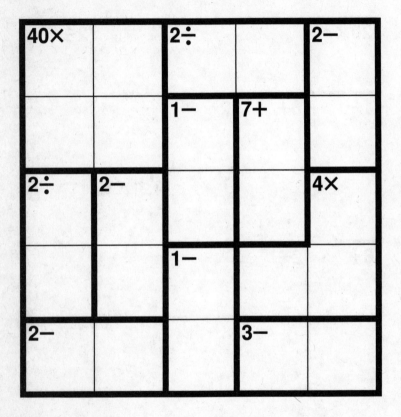

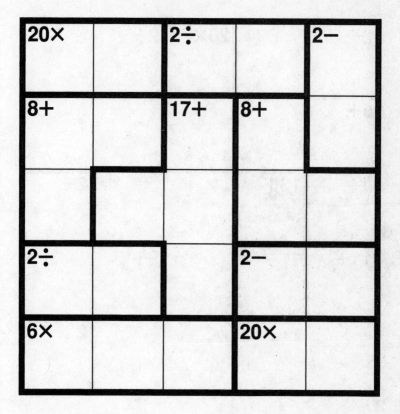

124 Very Challenging +/−/×/÷

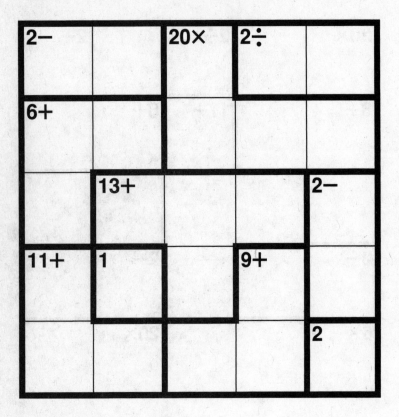

2−		20×	2÷	
6+				
	13+			2−
11+	1		9+	
				2

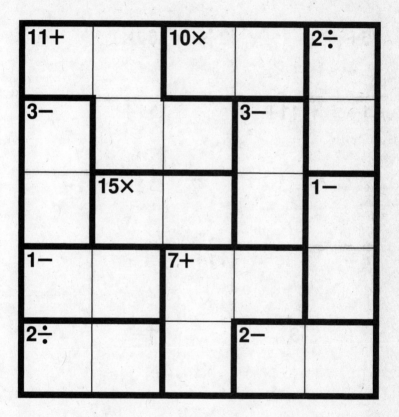

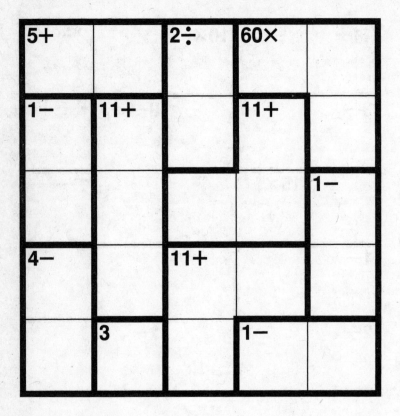

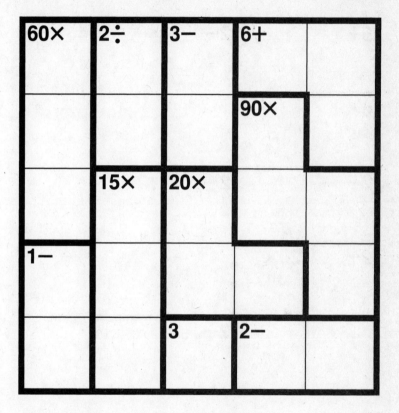

128 Very Challenging +/−/×/÷

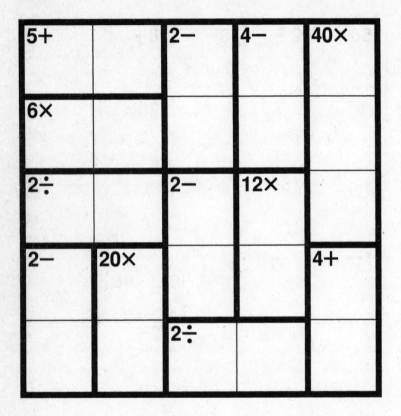

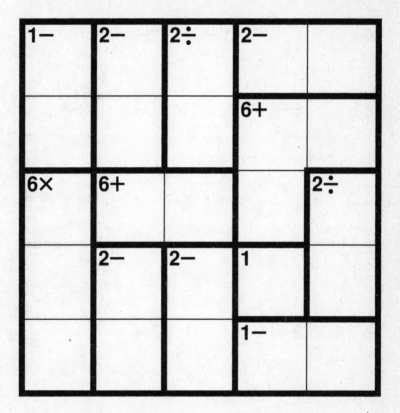

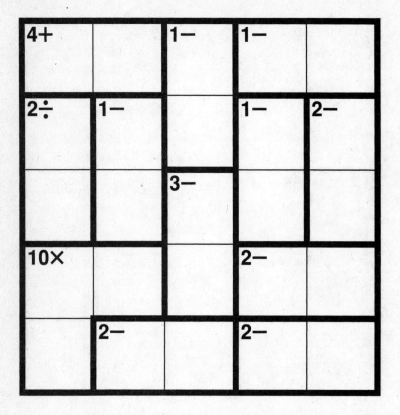

Very Challenging +/−/×/÷ 131

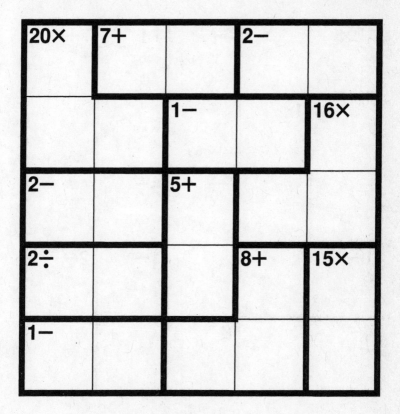

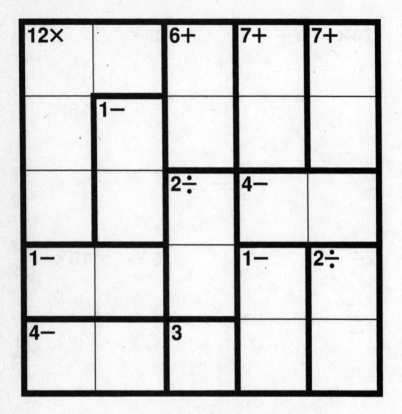

Very Challenging +/−/×/÷ 133

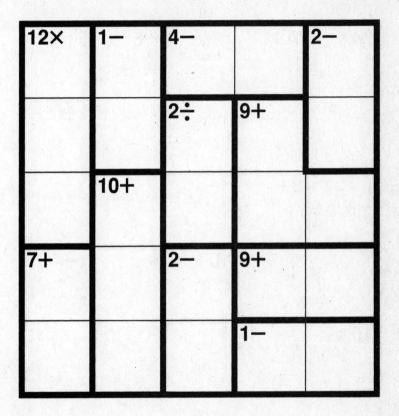

134 Very Challenging +/−/×/÷

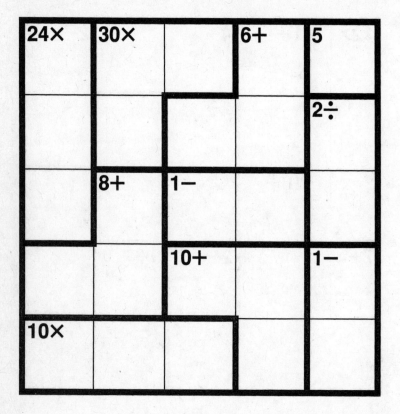

Very Challenging +/−/×/÷ 135

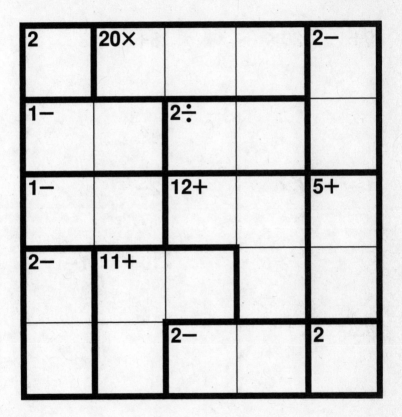

136 Very Challenging +/−/×/÷

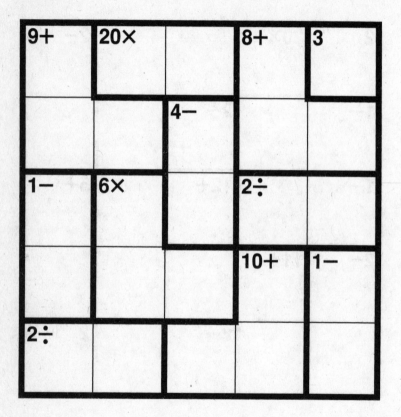

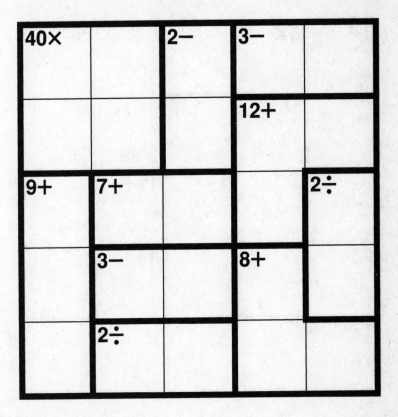

138 Very Challenging +/−/×/÷

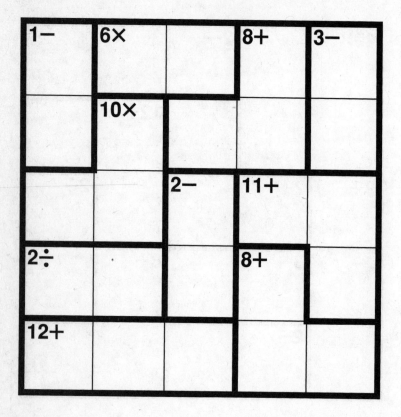

Very Challenging +/−/×/÷

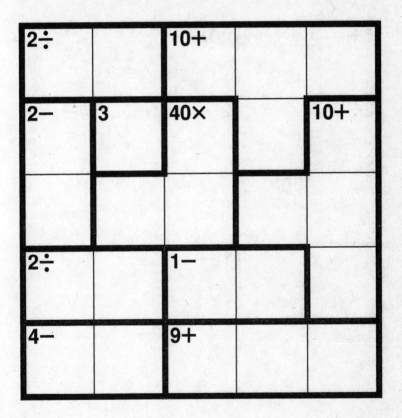

140 Very Challenging +/−/×/÷

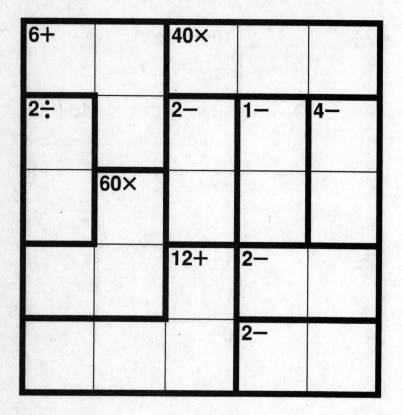

Very Challenging +/−/×/÷ 141

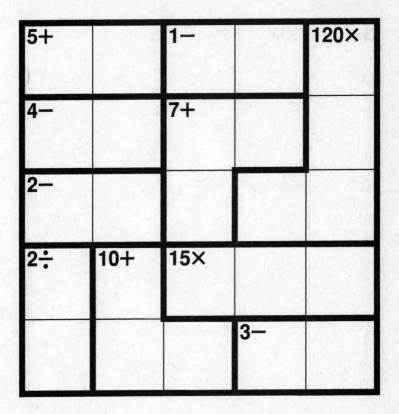

142 Very Challenging +/−/×/÷

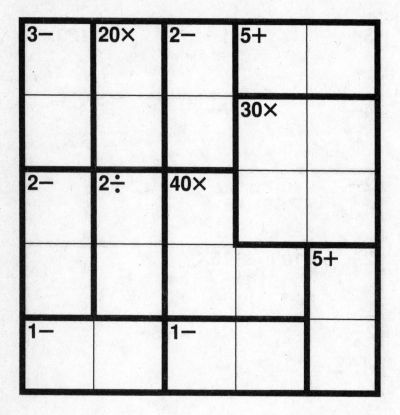

Very Challenging +/−/×/÷

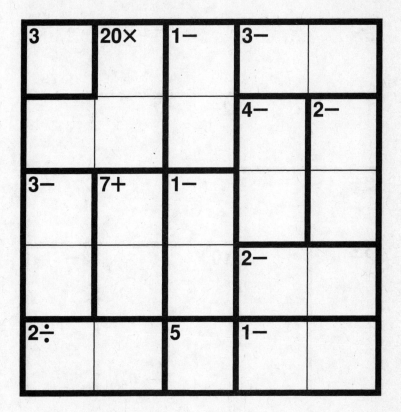

3	20×	1−	3−	
			4−	2−
3−	7+	1−		
			2−	
2÷		5	1−	

144 Very Challenging +/−/×/÷

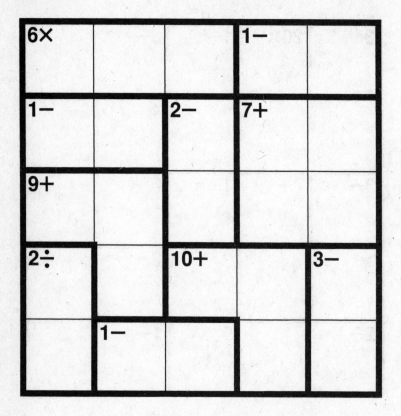

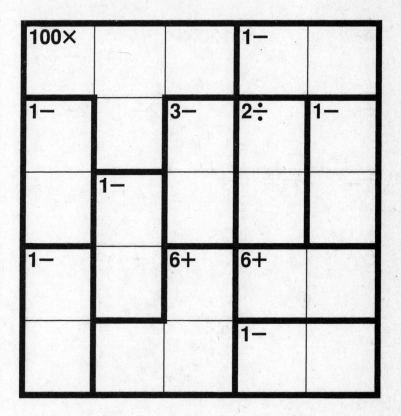

146 Very Challenging +/−/×/÷

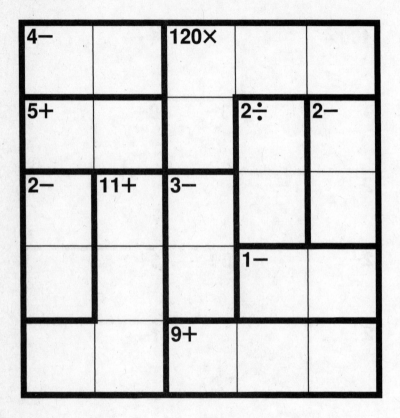

4−		120×		
5+			2÷	2−
2−	11+	3−		
			1−	
		9+		

Very Challenging +/−/×/÷

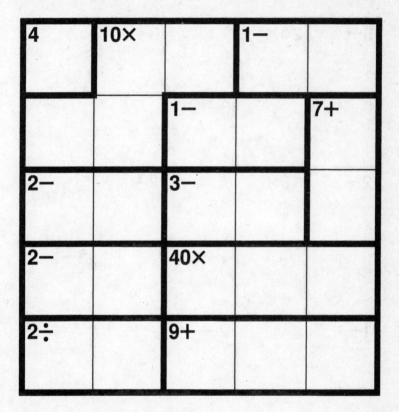

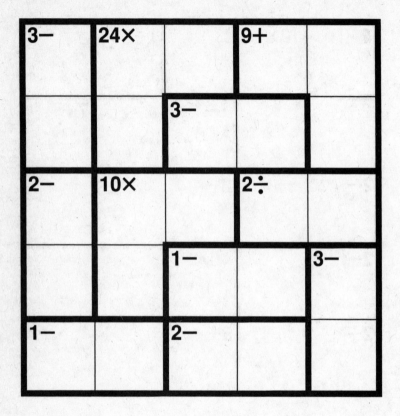

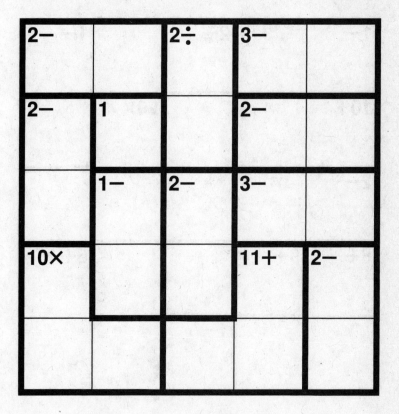

150 Very Challenging +/−/×/÷

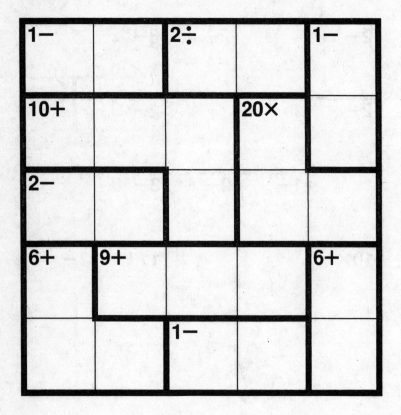

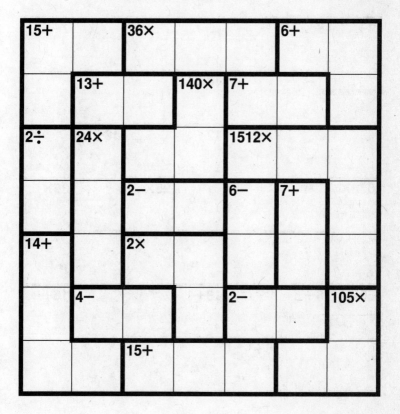

9+	84×			7+		7+
	1−		40×			
	2÷	2−	12+		13+	
672×				25×		36×
60×	6−		13+			16+
		6+				

Moderate +/−/×/÷ 153

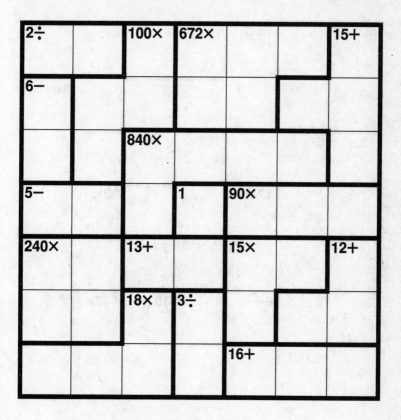

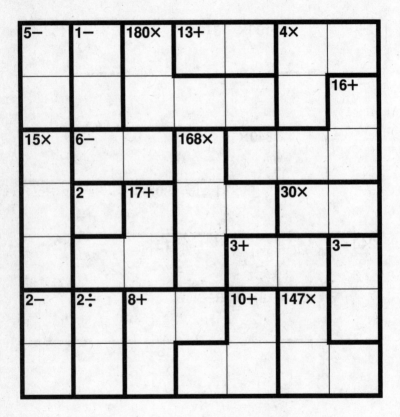

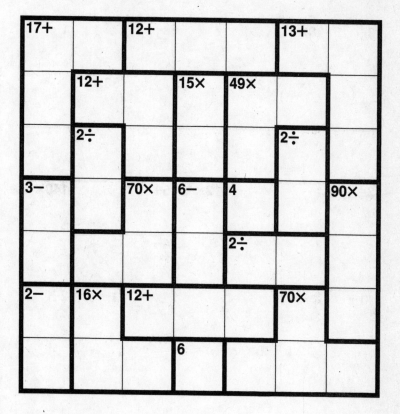

3÷	28×			8+		1−
	80×	12+			36×	
			7			
3÷	1−		12×	5+		140×
	2	2÷		4−		
11+	2−				1−	2÷
		40×				

7+	12+			12×		4−
	168×	3−			100×	
		3−				56×
3÷		5	9×		16+	
	3−	3+				
6+		9+		13+		2÷
	42×					

17+			6−		2÷	
	84×			20×		
16×		21×		14+	16+	2÷
42×		1−				
		3+				16+
12+	7	2÷				
		4	10×		4−	

2−	2÷	2÷		6−		2−
		15×		15+		
3+	10+	56×		210×		30×
			4			
2−			210×		3+	
1−	1−			3		8+
		1−		9+		

6−	18×	28×	3÷		3+	60×
			9+			
16+		60×	2÷	42×		
				10+		
	14+		20×	1−		8+
3÷		3÷			15+	
			4−			

15×		2÷		6−		72×
6×		4−		7+		
	14+			11+	60×	
3−		6	3+			6−
60×	24×					
		4−		1−		3−
9+		2÷		3−		

162 Moderate +/−/×/÷

1−		840×	4−		14×	
3+					2÷	
3−		144×			150×	
1	84×		1−		6−	
1−				84×		3+
	6×		14+			
12+					7+	

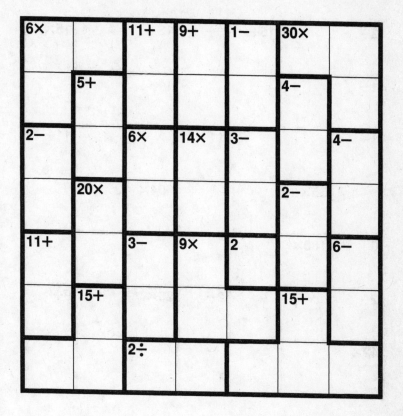

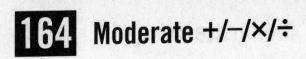

3÷		15+	3÷	13+		15×
1−				14×		
1−			11+			11+
	35×			504×	3	
6	180×					
2÷			2−	20×		9+
42×						

Moderate +/−/×/÷ 165

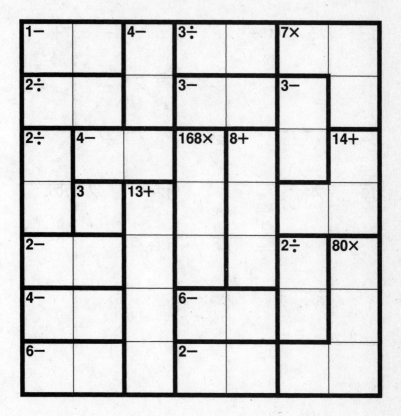

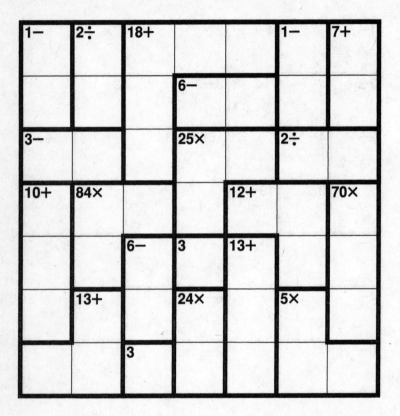

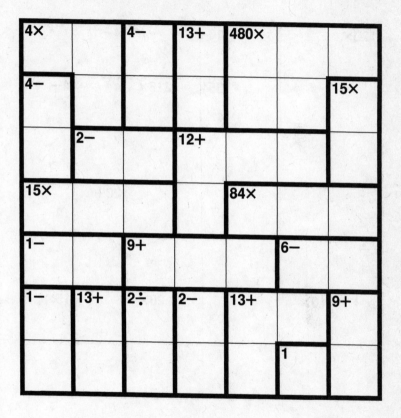

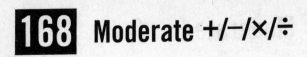

120×		3÷	13+		4−	
35×	216×	4	4−
	105×					
2÷				20+	
2÷		13+			
20+	16×			120×		15×

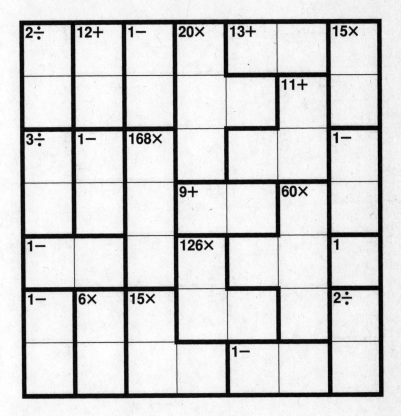

170 Moderate +/−/×/÷

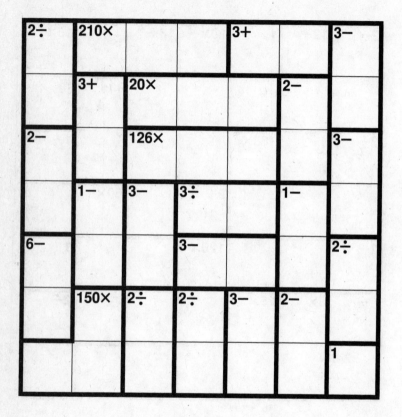

2÷	210×			3+		3−
	3+	20×			2−	
2−		126×				3−
	1−	3−	3÷		1−	
6−			3−			2÷
	150×	2÷	2÷	3−	2−	
						1

Moderate +/−/×/÷ 171

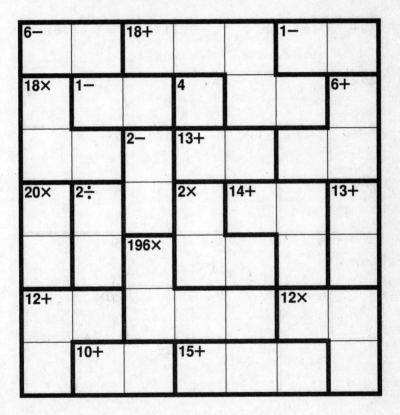

172 Moderate +/−/×/÷

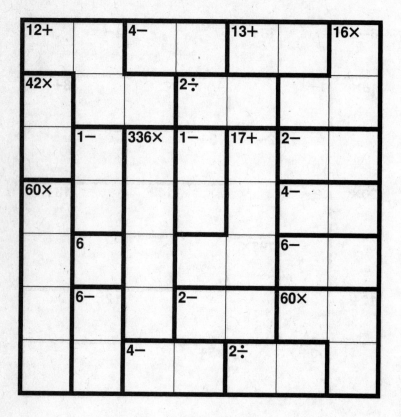

Moderate +/−/×/÷ 173

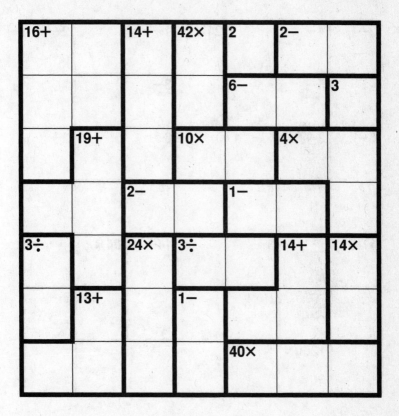

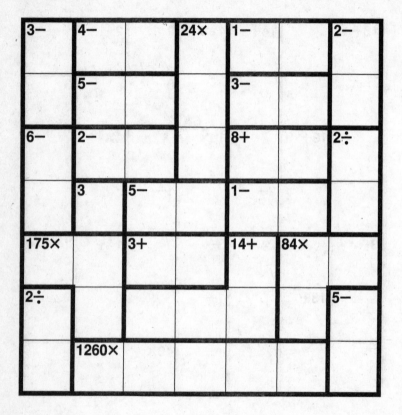

Moderate +/−/×/÷

6−		1440×		3÷		2−
2520×	5−		14+			
				16+		35×
	15+		3			
		28×			14+	
						21+
6+		7+				

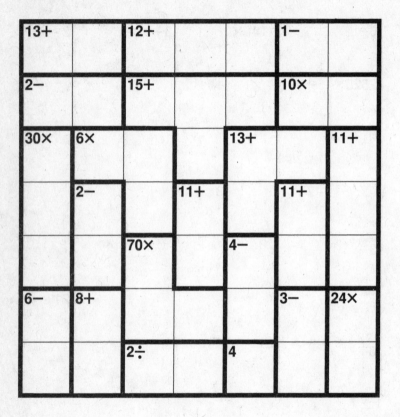

10×	8+	8+		14+		
		12×	28×		1−	3−
2÷				5		
	20×		36×		5−	
3−		4−			2−	1−
6−	3÷	1−	8×			
				60×		

178 Moderate +/−/×/÷

13+	420×		5−	2÷		1−
		20+			72×	
1−	28×		2÷		1	35×
	48×			15×		
1−		42×			5+	
12+			2÷		1−	

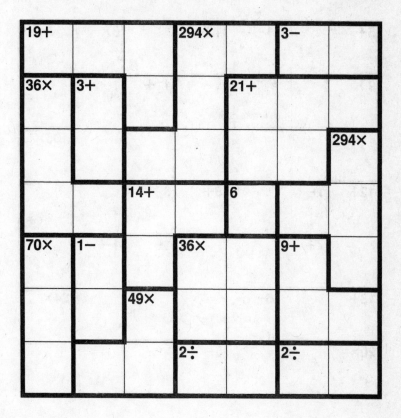

180 Moderate +/−/×/÷

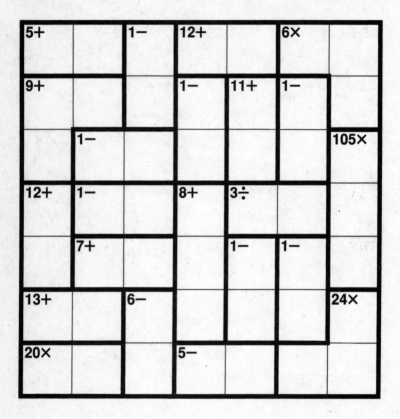

5+		1−	12+		6×	
9+			1−	11+	1−	
	1−					105×
12+	1−		8+	3÷		
	7+			1−	1−	
13+		6−				24×
20×			5−			

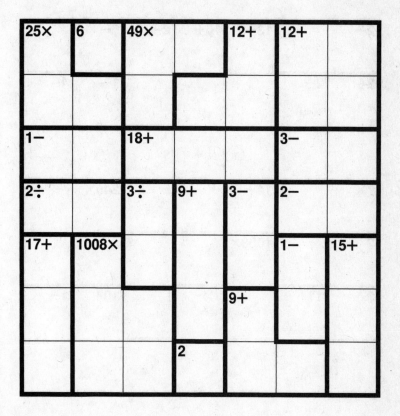

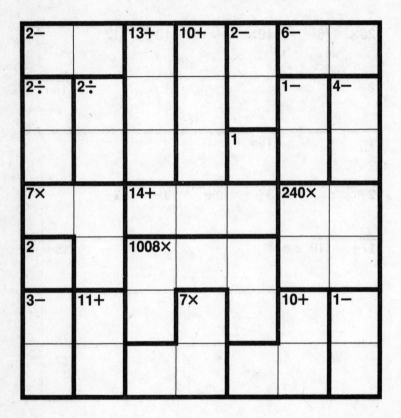

Moderate +/−/×/÷   183

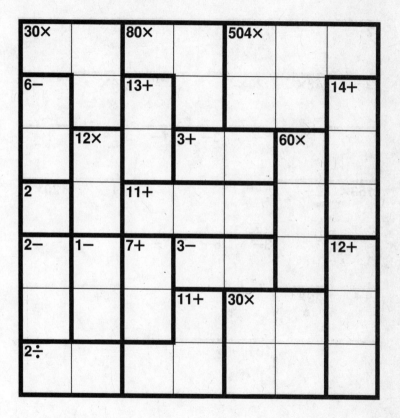

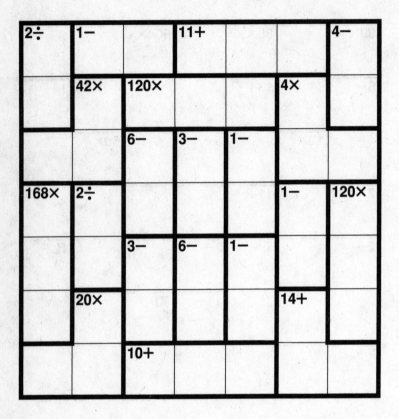

Moderate +/−/×/÷ 185

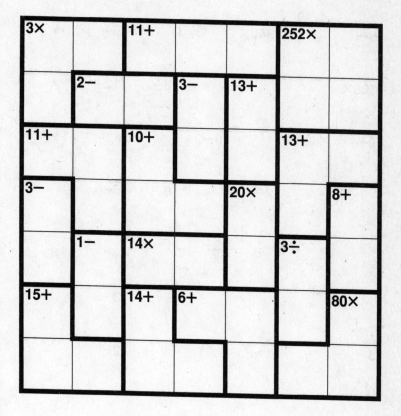

5−		840×			5+	
105×				3÷	12+	
9+	14+	1	6−			14+
		2÷		6	6−	
			2÷	2−		
14+					3−	
3−		11+			2−	

54×		56×			20×	
6		14+				
3+	2÷	18+			13+	4−
			1−			
6+		9+		2÷	2−	
2−			12×		1−	
3−					1−	

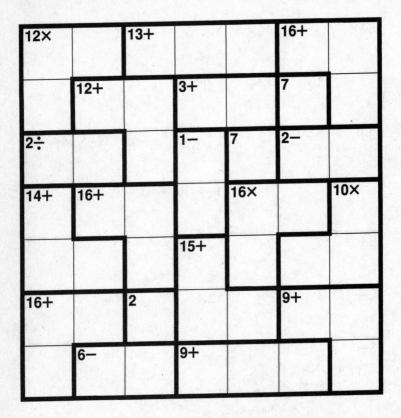

Moderate +/−/×/÷ 189

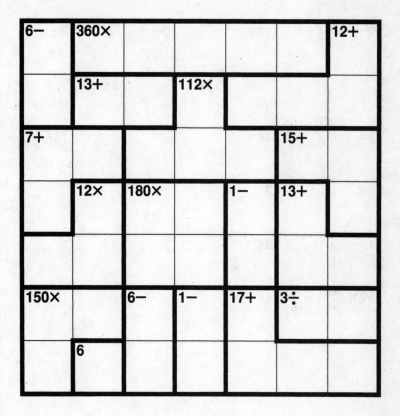

2−	4−	13+		3−		2÷
			13+		2−	
2÷		49×				15+
6×		2		20×		
1−		24×		2−	9+	
12×	1−	14+				7+
				13+		

12+	36×		6×		1−	
		8+		3−	11+	
1−		2−	168×		15+	
2÷				6		
13+		16×		12+		6×
1−	10+					
			2−		1−	

Moderate +/−/×/÷

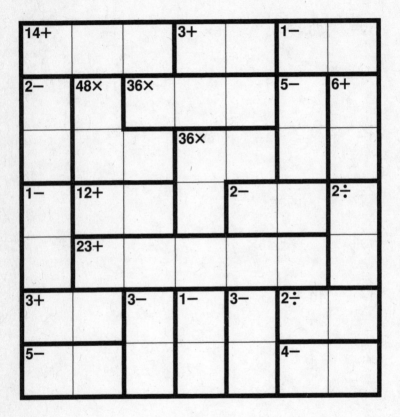

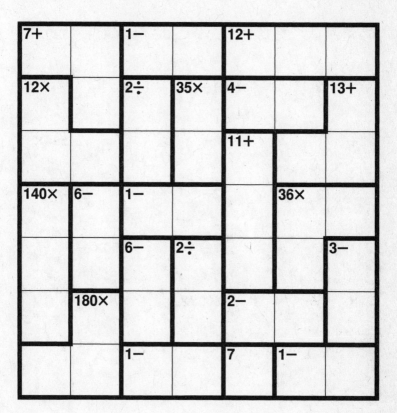

60×		13+		3÷		120×
	3−		3÷			
22+			2÷			504×
	3		2−			
	6−		3−		60×	
21×	1−		1008×			
		9+				

Demanding +/−/×/÷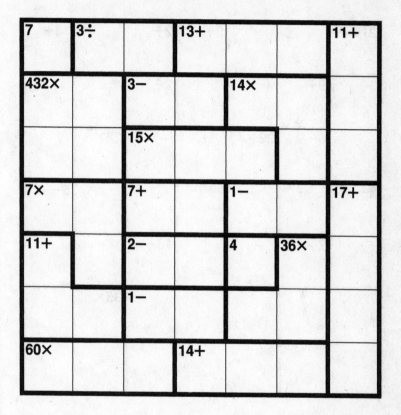

196 Demanding +/−/×/÷

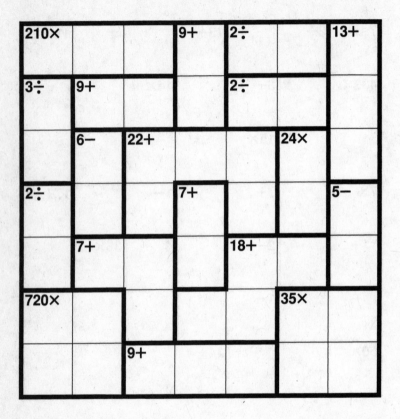

18+	9×		2−	16+		
		1		10+		1−
		2−	1−		175×	
2÷						
18+			2−	1−		1
13+	3−			6−		8+
		14+				

198 Demanding +/−/×/÷

3−		72×			8+	
140×	90×			1−		504×
		60×				
	2÷	84×			11+	
378×		28×	3÷	30×		
						12+
		28×				

Demanding +/−/×/÷ 199

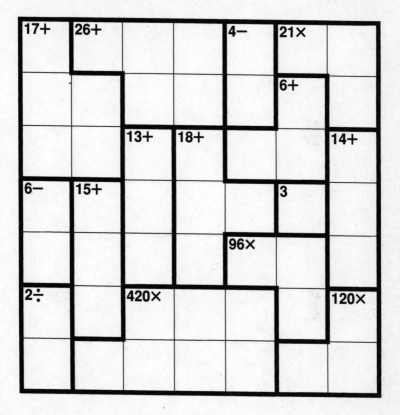

200 Demanding +/−/×/÷

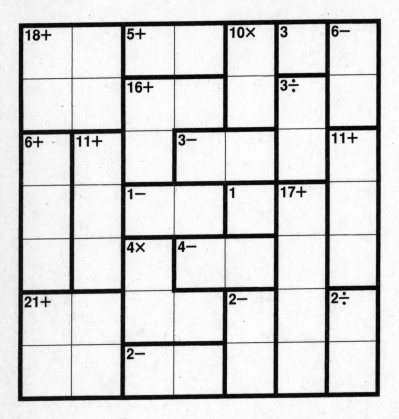

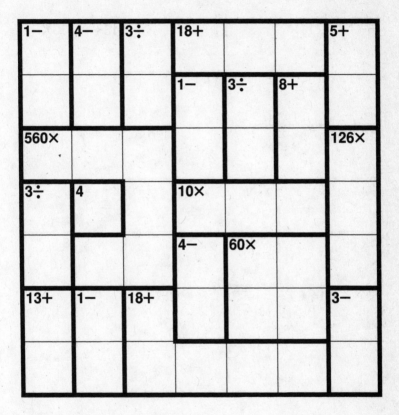

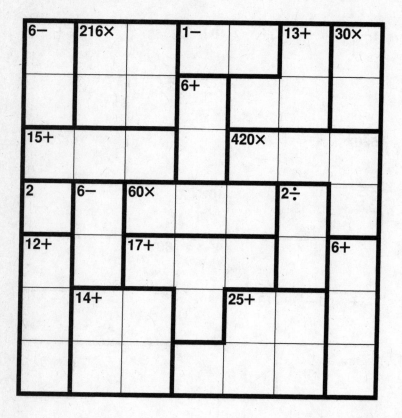

Demanding +/−/×/÷ 203

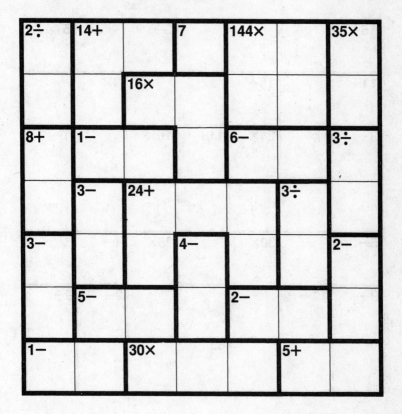

204 Demanding +/−/×/÷

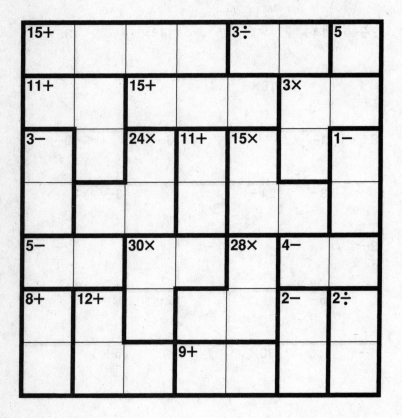

18+			6×	2÷	30×	
7+	12+					1−
		8+		1008×		
3−		1	4−			18+
6−	11+	2÷				
			1−	6+	14+	
11+						

120×	2	140×				16+
	2÷		10×			
	3−		6+			
6+	3−		13+	1−		8×
	3−			2−		
	20+	120×			14+	

16+		22+	4×		1−	
					5−	
		15+	24+		17+	2−
3÷			4			
	42×					15×
		120×		28×		
1−						3

208 Demanding +/−/×/÷

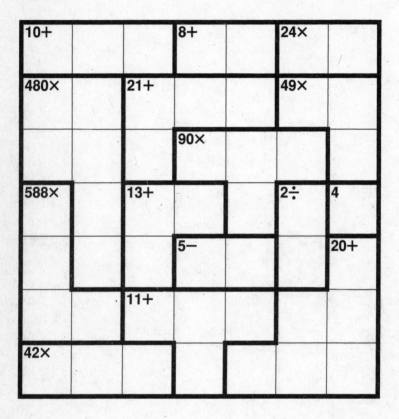

Demanding +/−/×/÷ 209

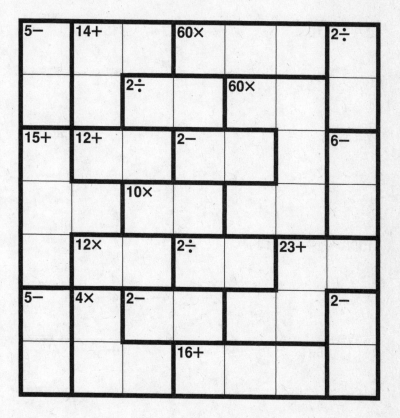

210 Demanding +/−/×/÷

2÷	10×		4−	7+	13+	
	18+	240×			14+	
2−						8+
				4−		
105×	1−	14+		3−		
			2÷	4−	4−	
	8+				9+	

Demanding +/−/×/÷ 211

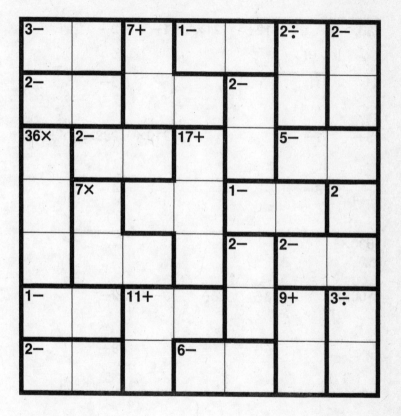

212 Demanding +/−/×/÷

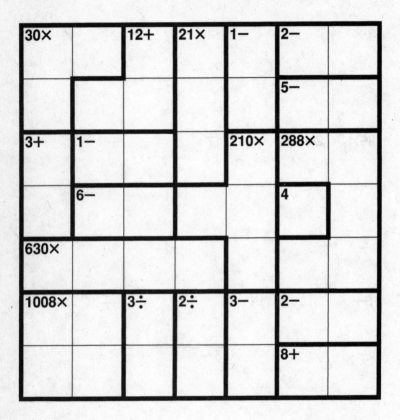

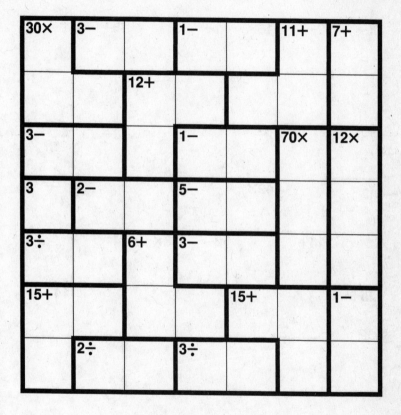

214 Demanding +/−/×/÷

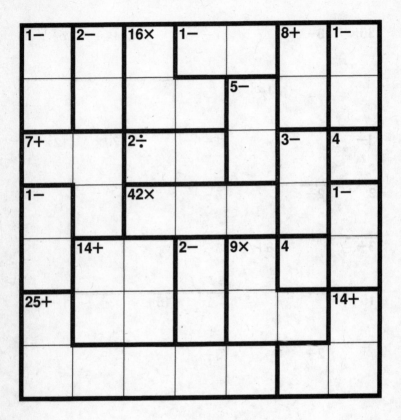

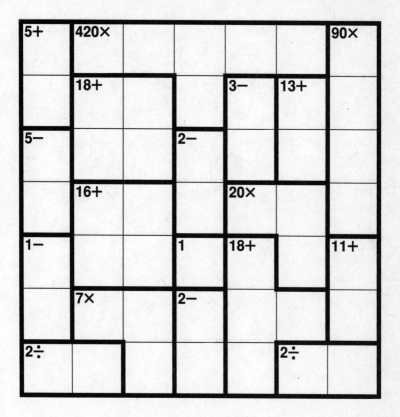

216 Demanding +/−/×/÷

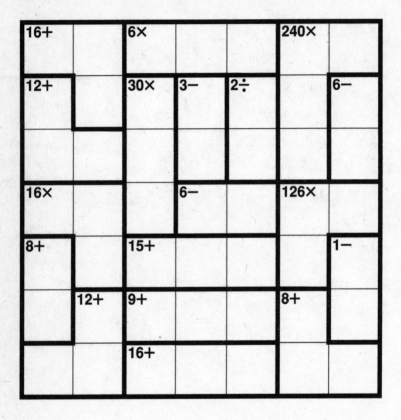

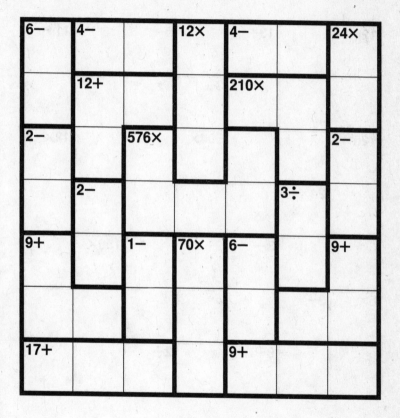

1260×		13+		6−		11+
			3−			
120×			504×			42×
	24×					
		3−	9+		150×	
6×	3−		5			
		8+		2÷		

Demanding +/−/×/÷ 219

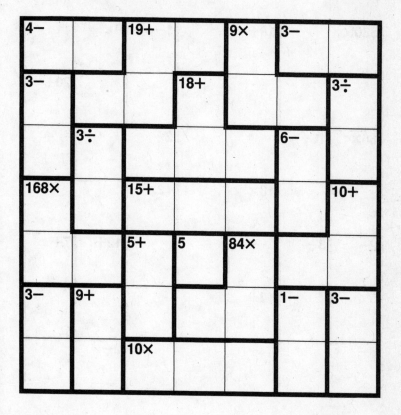

220 Demanding +/−/×/÷

560×		14+		1−	9×	
						20+
36×	16+			2÷		
		10×		12×		
2−	3÷				12+	7+
		12+				
6−		14+			2÷	

Demanding +/−/×/÷ 221

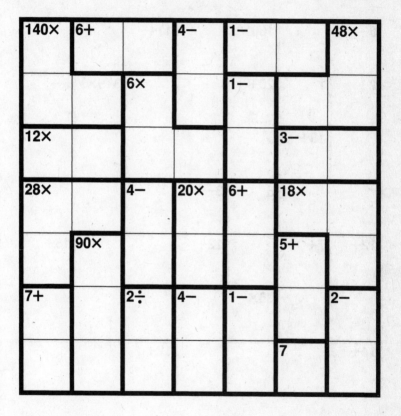

222 Demanding +/−/×/÷

6−		100×		11+		
2÷	1	20+			315×	5−
	13+					
		6	3−			
12+	7+		12+			15+
		36×				
14+			12+			

Demanding +/−/×/÷

2÷	16×		1−	13+		9+
		2÷		16+		
1−					3−	
1−		11+		1	1−	
35×	1−	20×			2÷	3÷
		11+				
20×			7	11+		

224 Demanding +/−/×/÷

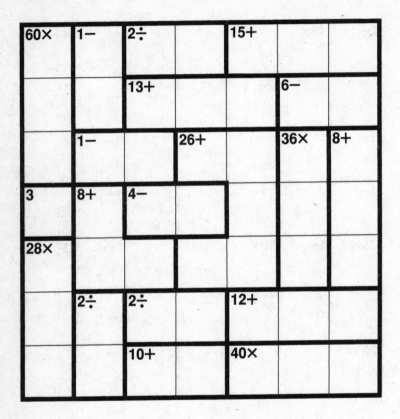

60×	1−	2÷		15+		
		13+			6−	
	1−		26+		36×	8+
3	8+	4−				
28×						
	2÷	2÷		12+		
		10+		40×		

5+	5	18+	13+		3÷	1−
	4×		4−			
			30×		14+	16+
21×			2÷			
16+			3−			
1−		84×	3−		72×	2÷
			1			

226 Demanding +/−/×/÷

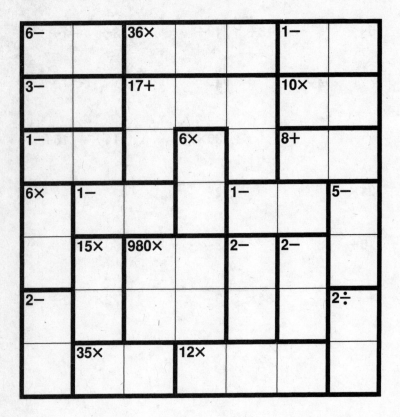

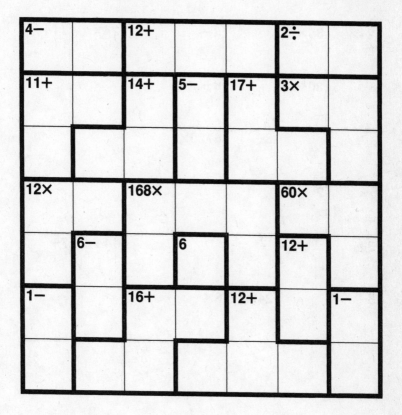

228 Demanding +/−/×/÷

24×	84×		3−		24×	11+
	20+		8+			
		3÷	6720×			
	2			42×		
8+					14+	7+
5−		24×	6×			
			4−			

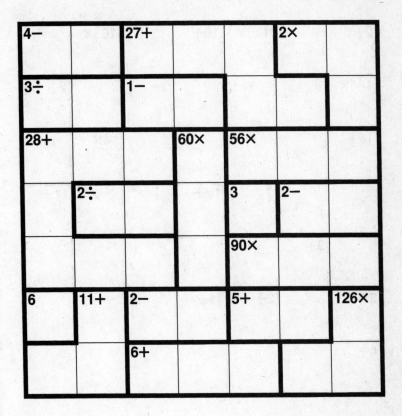

2÷		126×	10+		168×	
140×			3−		2÷	
18+				14×		
	7	18+			11+	
9+						
3÷	2÷	11+		9+		
4−						

Demanding +/−/×/÷ 231

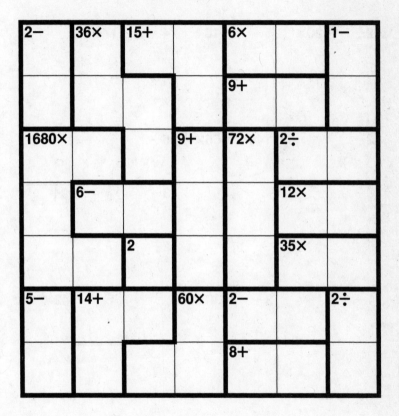

232 Demanding +/−/×/÷

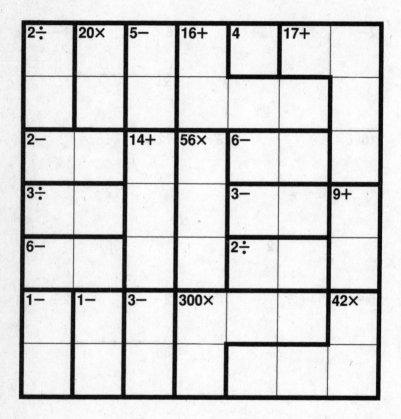

Demanding +/−/×/÷ 233

35×	6−	10+		1−		60×
			168×			
12+		210×		2÷		12×
	3		13+	4−		
2÷				3−		
1−	30×	9+			13+	
				10+		

234 Demanding +/−/×/÷

17+	3×		2−	18+		
					72×	
	245×		2−	8×		
17+	2÷				8+	4−
		48×				
		42×			1−	
3−		42×			1−	

Demanding +/−/×/÷ 235

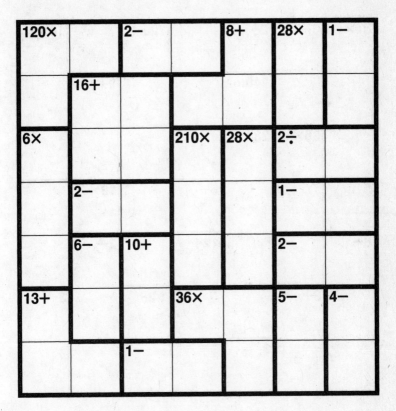

236 Demanding +/−/×/÷

84×	6−	2÷		120×		10×
		240×			9+	
	36×	28×				
5			5−		18×	
8+			12+		2−	
	9+			14+		3−
		3−				

4−	18+			1−		2÷
	840×		4×		20+	
21×						120×
			3			
2÷	1−		2−	2−		6−
	5−			2−		
2−		13+			1−	

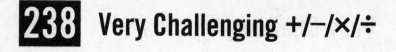

4−		40×	6−	10+	2÷	
14+						168×
	3+		2÷	2−		
	25+			5−		
			20+	3−		
13+	1				210×	
		9+				

Very Challenging +/−/×/÷ 239

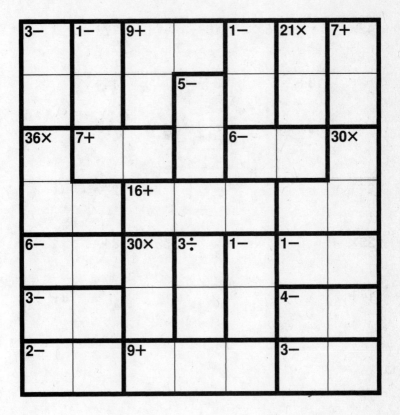

42×		8×	10+		17+	
	13+		3÷		14+	
			21+	4−		
2÷					2÷	
25×		14+		56×	8+	
14+						8+
			3−			

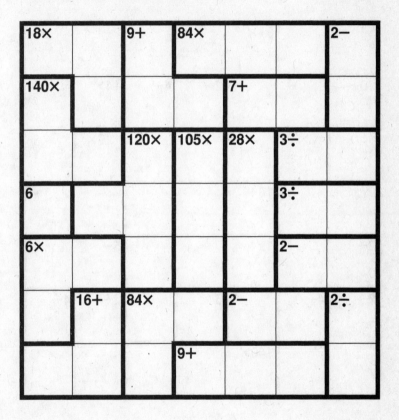

242 Very Challenging +/−/×/÷

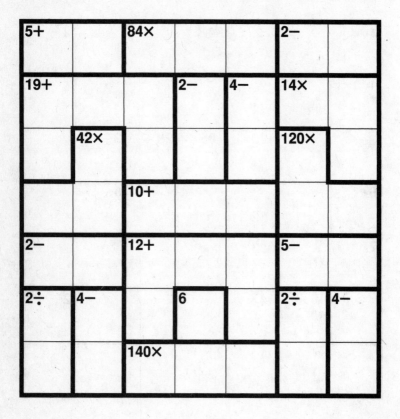

Very Challenging +/−/×/÷

4−	2÷		30×	1−		1−
	16+				80×	
3÷			3÷			2÷
	11+			1−		
7+		140×			12+	
	13+	15+			14×	
		11+				

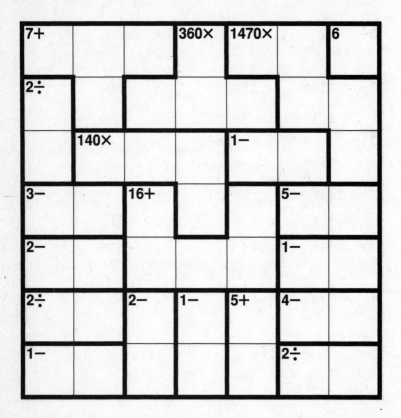

3÷		1−	16+	3−	2−	
3−					49×	
24+		56×				90×
				30×		
		1	14+		8+	
12×		11+		6×		
2−					2÷	

35×		19+			6×	
9+			4		16+	
	16+	11+			12+	
		12×	2−	4−		
2÷					14+	15×
	5+	16+				
6		40×				

Very Challenging +/−/×/÷ 247

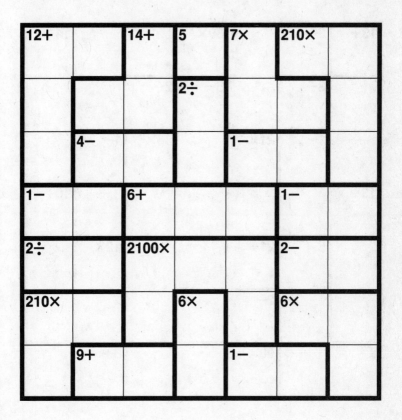

12+		14+	5	7×	210×	
			2÷			
	4−			1−		
1−		6+			1−	
2÷		2100×			2−	
210×			6×		6×	
	9+			1−		

248 Very Challenging +/−/×/÷

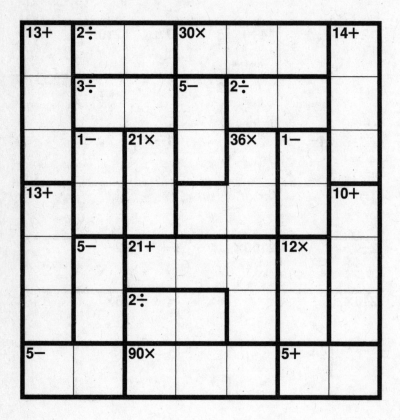

Very Challenging +/−/×/÷

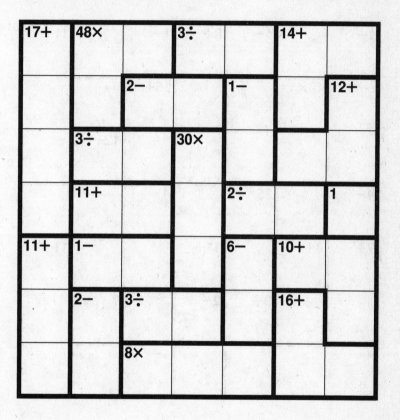

1−		4−	8+	1−		11+
5−	48×			15+		
					12+	
4−		25×		4		
7+	9+		11+			11+
		3÷	2−		7	
4−				1−		

Very Challenging +/−/×/÷

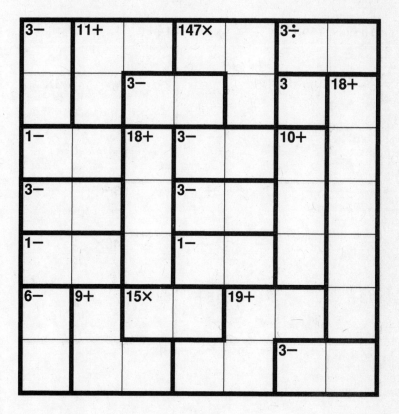

3−	11+		147×		3÷	
		3−			3	18+
1−		18+	3−		10+	
3−			3−			
1−			1−			
6−	9+	15×		19+		
					3−	

15+	144×			14+		
		12×		2−		40×
126×			6−			
	5+	5	2÷		3−	
		6−	2−		48×	
12+			15+	6+		
				42×		

Very Challenging +/−/×/÷

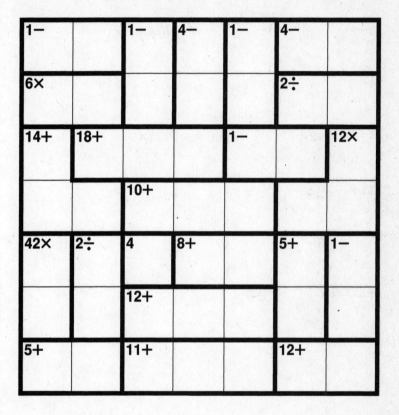

1−		1−	4−	1−	4−	
6×					2÷	
14+	18+			1−		12×
		10+				
42×	2÷	4	8+		5+	1−
		12+				
5+		11+			12+	

6−		1−		252×	2÷	
4−					11+	
4	12×		60×	490×		
11+					5	
	3−					180×
1−		26+				
9+		5+				

Very Challenging +/−/×/÷ 255

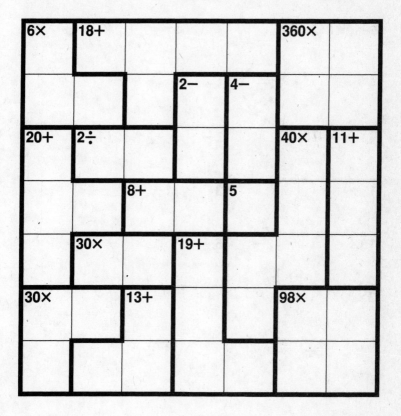

5880×	42×			1−		9+
		2÷	1−			
			2÷		21+	
13+			3	1−		
10×		2−	5−			
3×			14+		48×	
	2÷			11+		

Very Challenging +/−/×/÷ 257

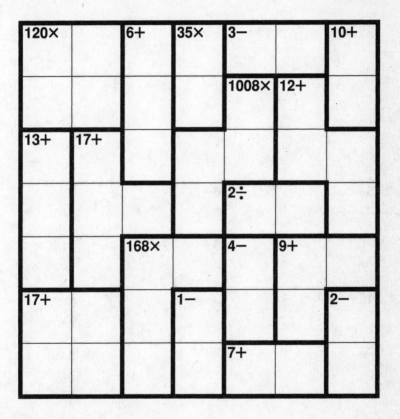

258 Very Challenging +/−/×/÷

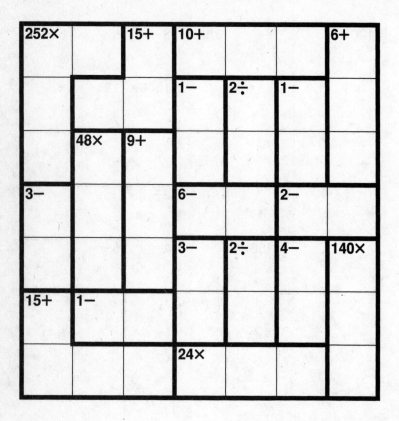

Very Challenging +/−/×/÷

1−	120×	15+			9+	3÷
11+		12×			5−	
30×			2−	11+		
5−		6×		630×	2−	
8+			2−		14+	

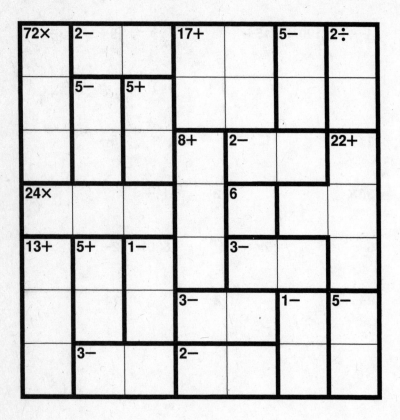

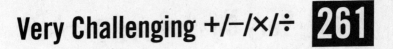

210×		18+	6+	560×	5−	
						2−
		23+				
84×					17+	
		2−		5−		
12×			35×		2÷	
	2−			3÷		1

5−		168×	1−	6+	15×	
2÷						3−
	42×	105×			13+	
		11+				
2−	7+		1−	3−		2÷
	30×			17+		
9+					2÷	

Very Challenging +/−/×/÷ 263

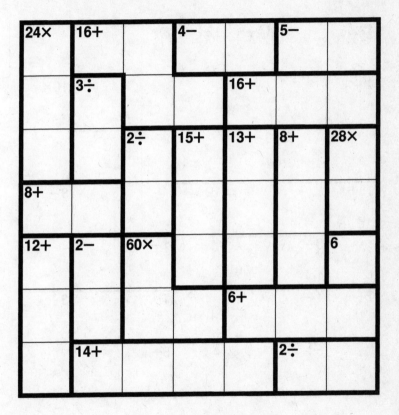

264 Very Challenging +/−/×/÷

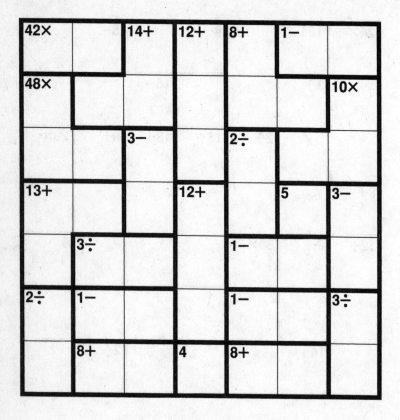

Very Challenging +/−/×/÷

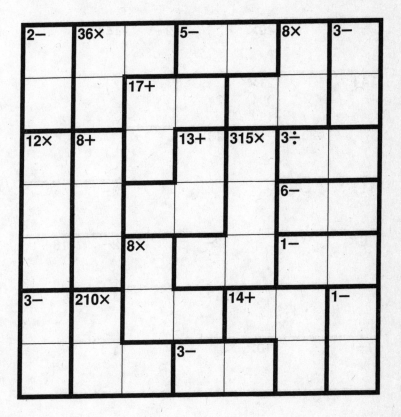

2÷		20×		2−	14+	
14+		21×			7+	
	420×		18×			
11+					2−	
20×			2−		2−	16+
			17+			
1−		10×			1	

84×		18+			2−	420×
		2÷				
120×	12×	10+	90×			
				8+		
				6	17+	
10+		3−		19+	2÷	
3−						

144×		12+			2÷	6−
		35×		15+		
30×		336×			2−	
	5				4−	
			8+	14+		11+
24+					2−	
		9+				

Very Challenging +/−/×/÷

1−		35×			3÷	
6+	5−		1−		5−	
	30×			26+		8+
2−		3÷			3	
2−	42×					
	3−		1−		2−	
1−		12×			7+	

270 Very Challenging +/−/×/÷

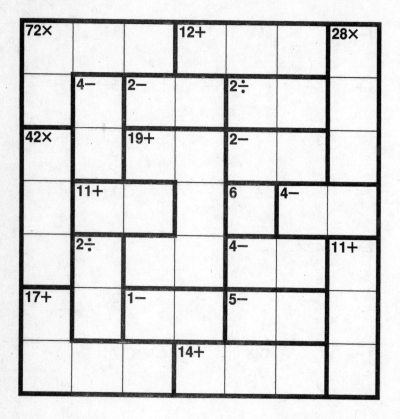

Very Challenging +/−/×/÷   271

30×		14+			9+	
	13+	10+			18+	
140×			2−			1
		2÷		10×	2÷	
126×					84×	
	210×	60×			96×	

272 Very Challenging +/−/×/÷

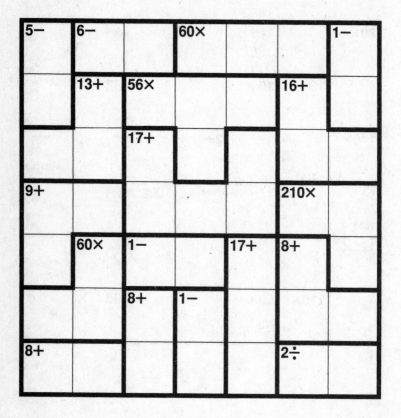

Very Challenging +/−/×/÷ 273

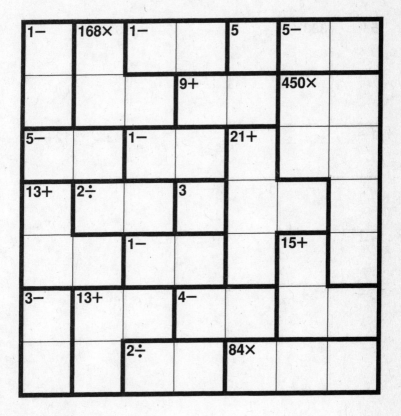

274 Very Challenging +/−/×/÷

5+	300×			504×	336×	
1−					42×	12+
3÷		10+	3−			
1−			12+	9+		
5−	18+				30×	
	3					

60×		5+	3−	3−	3−	
	2−				3−	3−
		22+				
21×	2÷		2		2÷	3−
		15+				
3−		1−	3÷	9+	42×	
2÷					2−	

276 Very Challenging +/−/×/÷

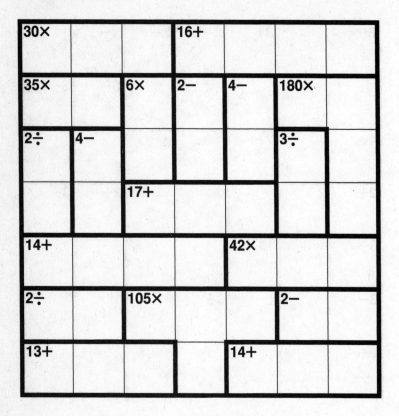

Very Challenging +/−/×/÷ 277

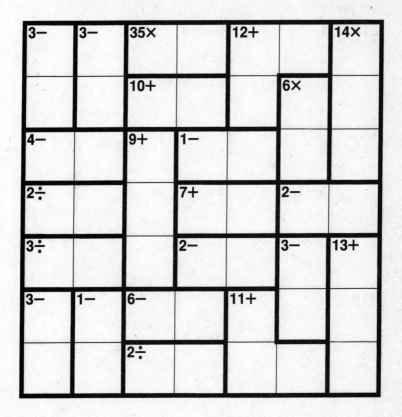

3−	3−	35×		12+		14×
		10+			6×	
4−		9+	1−			
2÷			7+		2−	
3÷			2−		3−	13+
3−	1−	6−		11+		
		2÷				

24×	1−		1−		3÷	
		10+	1−	12+		
105×				19+		2−
	5−		5+			
	30×		1−			2
11+				126×		
	5+		2−		5−	

Very Challenging +/−/×/÷ 279

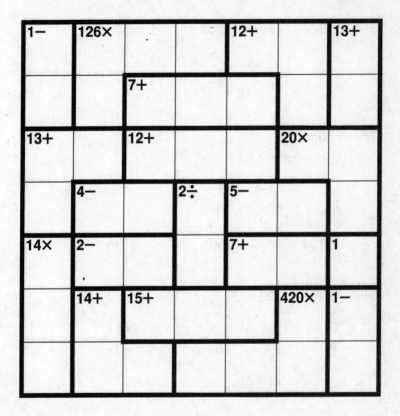

280 Very Challenging +/−/×/÷

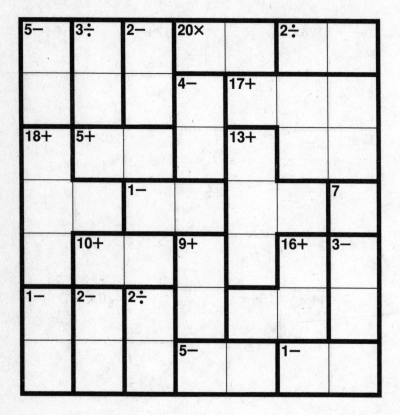

5−	3÷	2−	20×		2÷	
			4−	17+		
18+	5+			13+		
		1−				7
	10+		9+		16+	3−
1−	2−	2÷				
			5−		1−	

Very Challenging +/−/×/÷

840×			10+		10+	
		31+		2	60×	2−
13+			12+			
					6−	
2				72×		1−
8+			700×			
	2÷				5−	

24×		2−	5−		5−	
	15+		5+		2÷	
		2−		2−		8+
	4	1−		3÷		
42×		6×		3−		
42×		2−	3−		1−	
			2−		1−	

Very Challenging +/−/×/÷

2÷		60×	42×	26+		
3−						6+
	11+			8×		
4−	23+				21+	
18+			720×	84×		
					3	

3−	15×		4−		9+	9+
		16+		15+		
180×					12×	15+
		1				
15+		120×		35×		
	13+				4−	3÷
			1−			

Very Challenging +/−/×/÷

1680×			2÷		2÷	
			5−		1−	
60×	1−		126×	11+		
		10+		28×		1
				60×		
13+	14+		1−		2÷	
			1−		2÷	

90×			2÷	22+	5−	
13+		1−				
	4		12+	1−		
	17+			1	3−	
9+		2÷		3−		11+
			1−	1−		
12×					3−	

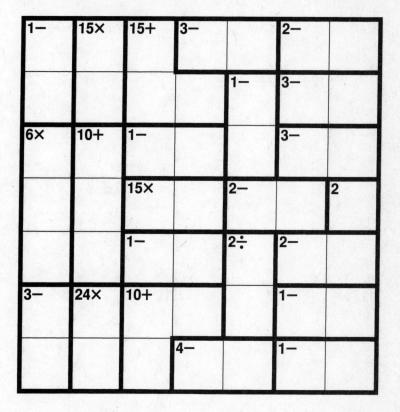

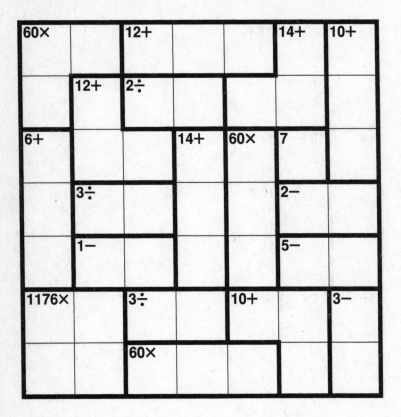

Very Challenging +/−/×/÷ 289

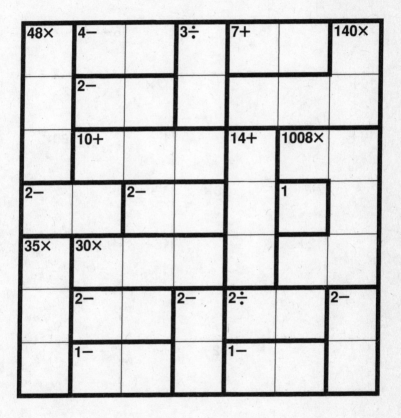

1−		36×			6−	
10+			15+	42×		
12+				1−		60×
	3−		6×	3÷		
	12+	5		10+	14+	
14+			2÷		2−	

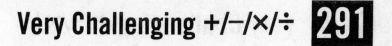

588×			15+	360×		
1−		420×	6+		3÷	
			13+	8+		3
12+	12×					140×
	60×	11+			17+	

292 Very Challenging +/−/×/÷

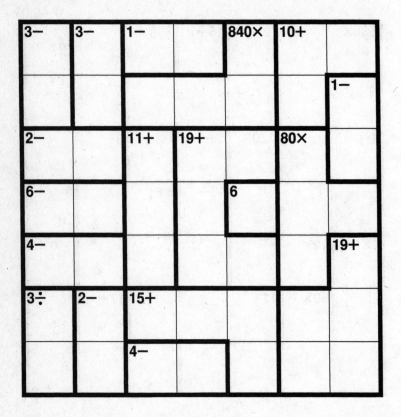

3−	3−	1−		840×	10+	
						1−
2−		11+	19+		80×	
6−			6			
4−						19+
3÷	2−	15+				
		4−				

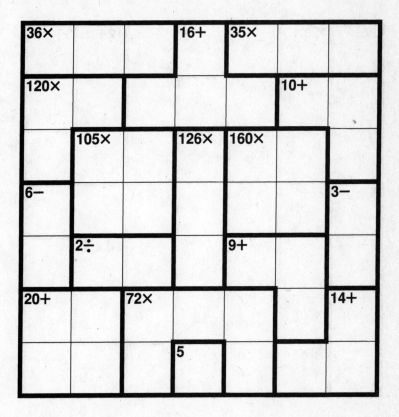

294 Very Challenging +/−/×/÷

17+	420×				12+	3÷
		17+		1−		
			17+			
6	27+			21×		
8+					60×	
						14+
	90×					

Very Challenging +/−/×/÷

84×	18+		16+			9+
			12+			
10+					10+	
	4−		14+	56×		
3÷					1−	
16+		84×			15×	
	1−		4	2÷		

8×	16+			15×		1−
	120×		15+			
		14+		17+	140×	
3						
1260×			12+		3÷	
		13+			30×	
				3−		

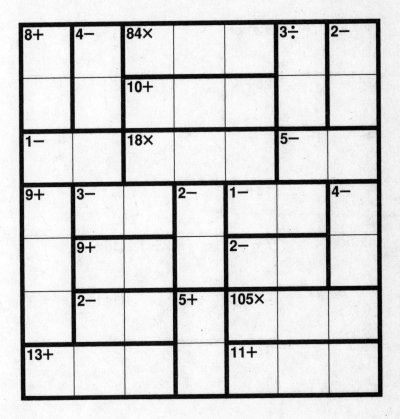

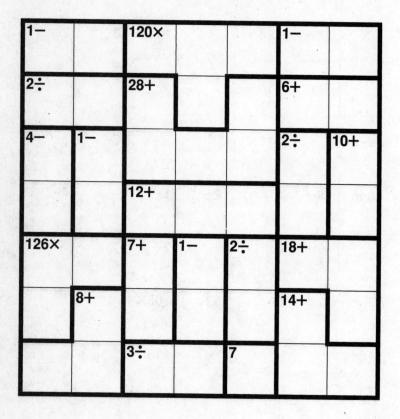

4−	3−		42×			1−
	14+			3÷		
210×			3÷	96×		
	2−			2−		
180×		24×			420×	
		10+				
24×		15+			2÷	

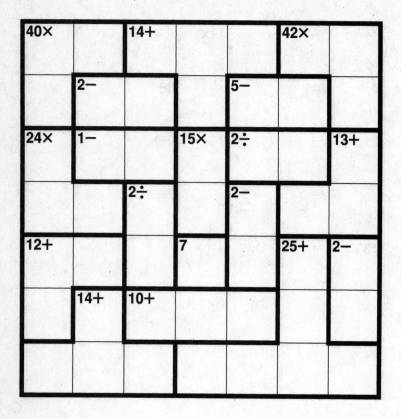

ANSWERS

1

12+ 5	**2−** 1	3	**1−** 2	**2÷** 4
1	**9+** 4	5	3	2
4	**90×** 5	**6+** 2	1	3
2	3	**3−** 1	4	**25×** 5
3	2	**4** 4	5	1

2

1− 4	**2÷** 1	**9×** 3	**3−** 2	5
5	2	1	3	**10+** 4
6+ 1	**60×** 3	5	4	2
3	4	**2÷** 2	**5** 5	**5+** 1
2	**5** 5	4	1	3

3

30× 5	3	**12+** 4	**1** 1	**3+** 2
2− 3	2	5	**9+** 4	1
1	**1−** 5	3	2	**4** 4
2÷ 2	4	**2×** 1	3	**75×** 5
4	1	2	5	3

4

3− 2	**4−** 5	**3−** 1	4	**7+** 3
5	1	**6×** 3	2	4
2÷ 4	2	**2−** 5	3	**1** 1
1− 3	4	**2÷** 2	**4−** 1	**10×** 5
2− 1	3	4	5	2

5

2÷ 4	2	75× 5	5+ 3	1
1− 2	5	3	1	4 4
3	4× 1	4	7+ 5	2
4− 5	9+ 4	1	1− 2	3
1	3	2	1− 4	5

6

5+ 3	7+ 2	5 5	5+ 4	1
2	5	5+ 4	2÷ 1	120× 3
2− 5	3	1	2	4
16× 4	1	8+ 3	5	2
1 1	4	1− 2	3	5

7

1− 4	5	2÷ 2	4+ 1	3
2÷ 2	1	4	2− 3	5
4+ 1	3	25× 5	2÷ 2	4
12+ 3	4	1	5	1− 2
5	6× 2	3	4 4	1

8

15× 5	1	3	2÷ 4	2
3+ 1	2÷ 2	4	60× 3	5
2	2− 3	5	1 1	4
4 4	60× 5	6+ 1	2	3
3	4	2 2	4− 5	1

9

9+ 2	**1−** 4	3	**4−** 5	1
5	2	**3×** 1	3	**2÷** 4
1− 4	**15×** 3	5	1	2
3	**5×** 1	**2÷** 4	**3−** 2	5
1	5	2	**1−** 4	3

10

8× 1	4	2	**2−** 5	3
10+ 2	3	**9+** 5	**3−** 1	4
5	**4−** 1	4	**18×** 3	**2÷** 2
1− 4	5	3	2	1
3	**2÷** 2	1	**9+** 4	5

11

3− 2	5	**3×** 1	**12×** 3	4
2− 5	1	3	**9+** 4	**1−** 2
3	**2÷** 2	4	5	1
3− 4	**3** 3	**8+** 2	1	5
1	**9+** 4	5	**1−** 2	3

12

3− 5	2	**1−** 4	**2−** 3	1
3× 3	1	5	**2÷** 4	2
1	**2÷** 4	2	**6+** 5	**60×** 3
2÷ 2	**15×** 5	3	1	4
4	**6+** 3	1	2	5

13

4^13+	**3**^9×	**5**^3−	**2**	**1**^1
2	**1**	**3**	**4**^60×	**5**
5	**2**	**4**^5+	**1**	**3**
3^3	**4**^20×	**1**^4−	**5**	**2**^2÷
1	**5**	**2**^1−	**3**	**4**

14

3^9+	**4**	**5**^15×	**1**	**2**^2÷
5^16+	**2**	**4**^16×	**3**	**1**
2	**5**	**1**	**4**	**3**^3
4	**1**^3×	**3**^1−	**2**^16+	**5**
1	**3**	**2**	**5**	**4**

15

3^60×	**4**	**1**	**2**^3−	**5**
4^2÷	**2**	**5**	**3**^8+	**1**
2^1−	**1**	**3**^3	**5**^9+	**4**
1^1	**5**^75×	**2**^2÷	**4**	**3**^6×
5	**3**	**4**	**1**	**2**

16

5^20×	**2**^2÷	**4**	**3**^7+	**1**
4	**1**	**2**^3−	**5**	**3**
1^9+	**3**	**5**	**2**^16×	**4**^4
3^9+	**5**^4−	**1**	**4**	**2**
2	**4**	**3**^3	**1**^6+	**5**

17

2− **3**	2÷ **2**	**4**	4− **1**	**5**
5	4 **4**	10+ **2**	**3**	2÷ **1**
4 **4**	4+ **3**	**1**	**5**	**2**
2× **2**	**1**	40× **5**	**4**	1− **3**
1	2− **5**	**3**	**2**	**4**

18

12× **3**	**1**	**4**	11+ **5**	**2**
2÷ **1**	1− **2**	**3**	**4**	10+ **5**
2	12× **3**	4− **5**	**1**	**4**
9+ **5**	**4**	10× **2**	3 **3**	**1**
4	**5**	**1**	6× **2**	**3**

19

2− **5**	1− **3**	6+ **1**	**4**	2÷ **2**
3	**2**	12+ **5**	**1**	**4**
10× **1**	**5**	**4**	2 **2**	2− **3**
2	16× **4**	**3**	75× **5**	**1**
4	**1**	2 **2**	**3**	**5**

20

4− **1**	**5**	1− **2**	12× **3**	**4**
5 **5**	6+ **1**	**3**	2÷ **4**	**2**
3	**2**	1− **4**	**5**	6+ **1**
2÷ **4**	1− **3**	2÷ **1**	**2**	**5**
2	**4**	5 **5**	4+ **1**	**3**

21

11+ 3	4	**3−** 2	**5×** 5	1
4	**30×** 2	5	1	**3** 3
5	3	1	**2÷** 2	4
4− 1	5	**1−** 3	4	**30×** 2
8× 2	1	4	3	5

22

15× 5	1	**1−** 3	2	**3−** 4
3	**2−** 5	**2÷** 2	**9+** 4	1
5+ 4	3	1	5	**10×** 2
1	**16×** 2	**60×** 4	3	5
2	4	5	1	**3** 3

23

1− 3	4	**15×** 1	**3−** 2	5
4− 1	3	5	**2÷** 4	2
5	**2÷** 1	**9+** 2	3	4
11+ 4	2	**60×** 3	5	**3×** 1
2	5	4	1	3

24

12× 1	4	**10+** 3	**3−** 2	5
3	5	2	**3−** 4	1
2÷ 4	2	**9+** 5	**7+** 1	3
4− 5	1	4	3	**2÷** 2
30× 2	3	1	5	4

25

4− 5	1− 4	1− 3	2	1− 1
1	5	24× 4	3	2
12× 3	2÷ 1	2	9+ 4	5
4	2	4− 1	5	7+ 3
10+ 2	3	5	1 1	4

26

2− 5	4+ 3	1	2÷ 4	2
3	11+ 5	2	2− 1	20× 4
2 2	4	30× 5	3	1
7+ 4	1 1	3	2	5
1	2	9+ 4	5	3 3

27

5+ 1	4	2÷ 2	2− 3	5
9+ 5	4+ 1	4	1− 2	3
4	3	9+ 1	20× 5	3+ 2
3− 2	5	3	4	1
1− 3	2	5	3− 1	4

28

2− 5	3	2÷ 2	3− 4	1
3+ 2	5	1	3	4
1	9+ 4	10× 5	2	1− 3
4	1	1− 3	5 5	2
6× 3	2	4	4− 1	5

29

4+ 1	3	**2÷** 4	2	**10×** 5
2÷ 4	**9+** 5	**2−** 1	3	2
2	4	**5** 5	**2−** 1	3
30× 5	2	**1−** 3	4	**10+** 1
3	**3+** 1	2	5	4

30

1− 4	**9×** 3	1	**5** 5	**4×** 2
5	**15+** 4	3	2	1
2− 1	2	4	**2−** 3	5
3	5	**2÷** 2	1	**11+** 4
10× 2	1	5	4	3

31

2÷ 2	1	**9+** 4	**15×** 3	5
1 1	2	3	**4−** 5	**1−** 4
1− 4	**10×** 5	2	1	3
3	**12+** 4	**4−** 5	**1−** 2	1
5	3	1	**2÷** 4	2

32

4− 1	**30×** 3	2	5	**14+** 4
5	**7+** 4	3	**1** 1	2
2÷ 2	**3−** 1	4	3	5
4	**6+** 5	1	**6+** 2	3
5+ 3	2	**1−** 5	4	1

33

100× **5**	**4**	2− **3**	2÷ **1**	**2**
3+ **2**	**5**	**1**	1− **4**	7+ **3**
1	1− **3**	**2**	**5**	**4**
2− **3**	**1**	20× **4**	1− **2**	6+ **5**
2÷ **4**	**2**	**5**	**3**	**1**

34

2÷ **2**	3× **1**	**3**	1− **4**	2− **5**
4	9+ **2**	**1**	**5**	**3**
4− **5**	**4**	2 **2**	1− **3**	7+ **1**
1	**3**	1− **5**	**2**	**4**
8+ **3**	**5**	**4**	1 **1**	**2**

35

13+ **5**	**3**	**4**	2÷ **1**	**2**
1	15+ **2**	**5**	**3**	4 **4**
12+ **4**	**1**	4× **2**	**5**	2− **3**
3	**4**	**1**	**2**	**5**
3− **2**	**5**	3 **3**	5+ **4**	**1**

36

1− **3**	20× **4**	**5**	**1**	24× **2**
2	2− **1**	**3**	5 **5**	**4**
4− **1**	**5**	4 **4**	8+ **2**	**3**
8+ **5**	**3**	**2**	**4**	4− **1**
2÷ **4**	**2**	2− **1**	**3**	**5**

37

2÷ 2	1	**2−** 5	**9+** 4	3
16× 1	4	3	2	**3−** 5
4	**10+** 5	**4+** 1	3	2
10+ 5	3	2	**20×** 1	**4** 4
3	2	4	5	1

38

25× 1	5	**9+** 2	3	4
5	**11+** 3	4	**2÷** 1	2
2− 4	**5+** 1	3	**3−** 2	5
2	4	1	**9+** 5	3
5+ 3	2	**9+** 5	4	1

39

7+ 2	**4−** 5	1	**60×** 3	**4** 4
3	2	4	5	**2÷** 1
9+ 4	**2−** 3	5	**8+** 1	2
5	**2÷** 1	2	4	3
8+ 1	4	3	**3−** 2	5

40

30× 2	**8+** 3	5	**2−** 1	**5+** 4
5	**2÷** 4	2	3	1
3	**15×** 5	1	**2÷** 4	2
5+ 4	**2÷** 1	3	**40×** 2	**2−** 5
1	2	4	5	3

41

1− 3	2− 5	2÷ 2	4	4× 1
2	3	5 5	1	4
3− 4	2÷ 2	1	7+ 5	2− 3
1	1− 4	3	2	5
4− 5	1	1− 4	3	2 2

42

1− 3	2	1− 4	1	1− 5
5× 1	5	3	2	4
15+ 2	1	1− 5	4	9× 3
5	4	2÷ 2	3	1
4	3 3	1	3− 5	2

43

13+ 4	2	15× 5	1	3
2	5	1− 4	3	1 1
36× 3	4	2÷ 1	40× 5	2
4− 1	3	2	4	40× 5
5	2− 1	3	2	4

44

1− 4	5	40× 2	2− 1	1− 3
2÷ 1	4	5	3	2
2	2÷ 1	12+ 3	5	4
45× 3	2	3− 1	4	4− 5
5	3	2− 4	2	1

45

$^{4-}$ 5	$^{60\times}$ 3	4	$^{2\div}$ 2	1
1	5	$^{10+}$ 2	$^{1-}$ 4	3
$^{8\times}$ 4	1	3	5	^{2} 2
2	$^{3-}$ 4	1	$^{8+}$ 3	5
$^{1-}$ 3	2	$^{20\times}$ 5	1	4

46

$^{2-}$ 1	3	$^{2\div}$ 4	2	$^{30\times}$ 5
$^{1-}$ 4	5	$^{4+}$ 1	3	2
$^{2-}$ 2	4	$^{4-}$ 5	1	3
$^{8+}$ 5	$^{8+}$ 2	3	$^{3-}$ 4	1
3	1	2	$^{1-}$ 5	4

47

$^{1-}$ 4	5	$^{2\div}$ 1	2	$^{1-}$ 3
$^{15\times}$ 5	3	$^{5+}$ 4	1	2
$^{2\div}$ 1	2	$^{1-}$ 3	4	$^{1-}$ 5
$^{6\times}$ 2	$^{5+}$ 1	$^{2-}$ 5	3	4
3	4	^{2} 2	$^{6+}$ 5	1

48

$^{2\div}$ 2	$^{30\times}$ 3	5	$^{3-}$ 1	4
4	2	$^{3-}$ 1	$^{10+}$ 3	5
$^{15\times}$ 3	1	4	$^{7+}$ 5	2
5	$^{24\times}$ 4	3	2	$^{8+}$ 1
$^{4-}$ 1	5	2	4	3

49

10× 5	5+ 2	1− 4	4+ 1	3
2	3	5	24× 4	1 1
1− 4	5	2÷ 1	3	2
2− 3	3− 1	2	1− 5	4
1	4	30× 3	2	5

50

2− 3	1	2÷ 2	10× 5	9+ 4
1− 4	3	1	2	5
7+ 5	1− 4	3	2÷ 1	2
2	8+ 5	36× 4	3	1
1	2	1− 5	4	3

51

1− 5	1− 4	5× 1	7+ 2	3
4	3	5	1	2
2÷ 1	2	1− 3	4	4− 5
1− 2	1− 5	4	15× 3	1
3	2÷ 1	2	5	4 4

52

8+ 2	5	1− 4	9× 3	1
4 4	1	5	2÷ 2	3
10+ 3	4	8× 2	1	10× 5
6+ 5	3	1	4	2
1	1− 2	3	1− 5	4

53

3− **1**	**4**	40× **5**	**2**	2− **3**
10+ **5**	**2**	**4**	1− **3**	**1**
3	1− **1**	**2**	**4**	100× **5**
2÷ **2**	8+ **3**	2− **1**	**5**	**4**
4	**5**	**3**	2÷ **1**	**2**

54

2÷ **2**	1 **1**	1− **4**	**5**	2− **3**
1	120× **2**	**3**	**4**	**5**
7+ **4**	2− **3**	**5**	2÷ **1**	**2**
3	**5**	6+ **1**	**2**	5+ **4**
5 **5**	2÷ **4**	**2**	**3**	**1**

55

7+ **2**	**3**	2− **5**	16× **1**	**4**
8× **1**	**2**	**3**	**4**	14+ **5**
4	**1**	**2**	**5**	**3**
2− **3**	1− **5**	2÷ **4**	**2**	**1**
5	**4**	6× **1**	**3**	**2**

56

2÷ **2**	**1**	1− **5**	**4**	2− **3**
20× **5**	**4**	1− **2**	**3**	**1**
2− **3**	5+ **2**	3− **1**	3− **5**	4 **4**
1	**3**	**4**	**2**	10× **5**
4 **4**	2− **5**	**3**	**1**	**2**

57

30× 5	3	5+ 4	1	2÷ 2
1	2	1− 3	10+ 5	4
6× 3	9+ 5	2	4	1
2	4	4− 1	1− 3	2− 5
5+ 4	1	5	2	3

58

2− 3	2÷ 2	4	4− 5	1
5	4 4	2÷ 2	1	7+ 3
2÷ 1	30× 3	5	2	4
2	20× 1	2− 3	1− 4	5
4	5	1	1− 3	2

59

8× 4	1	2	2− 3	5
8+ 2	3	5+ 4	6+ 5	1
3	5 5	1	7+ 4	2
4− 5	2÷ 2	30× 3	1	1− 4
1	4	5	2	3

60

15× 5	1	8+ 4	3	2 2
3	40× 2	1	9+ 4	5
4	5	3 3	1− 2	1
2÷ 2	14+ 3	5	3− 1	4
1	4	2	2− 5	3

61

$2\div$ 1	2	$1-$ 3	$2-$ 5	$3-$ 4
$20\times$ 5	4	2	3	1
$5+$ 3	$4-$ 1	$3-$ 4	2 2	$2-$ 5
2	5	1	$12+$ 4	3
$1-$ 4	3	5	1	2

62

$5\times$ 5	1	$1-$ 4	$2-$ 3	$8\times$ 2
1	$1-$ 2	3	5	4
$2\div$ 4	3	$8+$ 5	2	1
2	$12+$ 5	1	$1-$ 4	3
3	4	2 2	$4-$ 1	5

63

$1-$ 2	3	$1-$ 4	$6+$ 5	$3-$ 1
$1-$ 5	$2\div$ 2	3	1	4
4	1	$6\times$ 2	3	$30\times$ 5
$12\times$ 1	4	$40\times$ 5	2	3
3	5 5	1	4	2

64

$3-$ 4	$7+$ 5	$2\div$ 1	2	$12\times$ 3
1	2	$2-$ 3	5	4
$2-$ 3	1	$3-$ 2	$1-$ 4	5
$40\times$ 2	4	5	$2-$ 3	$2\div$ 1
5	$1-$ 3	4	1	2

65

¹²⁺5	²⁴ˣ3	²÷2	4	⁵⁺1
4	2	⁵5	1	3
3	4	¹⁻1	2	¹¹⁺5
⁶⁺1	5	¹⁻4	²⁻3	2
¹⁻2	1	3	5	4

66

²⁴ˣ2	3	⁸⁺5	1	¹⁻4
4	⁶⁺1	3	2	5
¹⁻5	4	2	²⁻3	1
⁴⁺1	²÷2	4	²⁰ˣ5	¹⁻3
3	⁴⁻5	1	4	2

67

¹²⁺4	5	1	²⁴ˣ2	3
²⁻3	1	2	¹⁵ˣ5	4
⁵5	¹⁻3	¹⁻4	1	²÷2
⁴ˣ2	4	5	3	1
1	2	¹²⁺3	4	5

68

¹⁻1	¹⁻3	4	¹⁰ˣ5	2
2	²÷1	²⁻3	⁴4	¹⁻5
¹⁻3	2	5	⁶⁺1	4
4	⁹⁺5	2	3	²⁻1
⁵5	4	²÷1	2	3

69

1− 3	4− 5	2÷ 4	2	2÷ 1
4	1	30× 5	3	2
24× 2	4	1	8+ 5	3
8+ 1	3	2	4 4	1− 5
5	2	2− 3	1	4

70

3− 1	40× 2	4	2− 3	5
4	5	2÷ 2	2− 1	3
10+ 3	3− 4	1	3− 5	2
5	1	1− 3	2	3− 4
2	12+ 3	5	4	1

71

10× 1	2− 3	10× 2	5	5+ 4
2	5	11+ 3	4	1
5	2÷ 2	4	2− 1	3
1− 3	4	10× 1	2	5
4	4− 1	5	1− 3	2

72

3− 1	4	30× 5	3	2
2÷ 2	8+ 5	12× 3	4	1
4	2	1	8+ 5	12+ 3
4+ 3	1	2− 4	2	5
2− 5	3	2	1	4

73

4 (1−)	**5**	**1** (2÷)	**2** (120×)	**3**
3 (5+)	**1** (2−)	**2**	**4**	**5**
2	**3**	**4** (1−)	**5**	**1** (7+)
5 (4−)	**2** (6+)	**3**	**1**	**4**
1	**4** (12+)	**5**	**3**	**2**

74

4 (2÷)	**2**	**3** (2−)	**5** (9+)	**1** (1)
2 (6×)	**5** (5)	**1**	**4**	**3** (1−)
1	**3**	**5** (1−)	**2** (12×)	**4**
5 (13+)	**1**	**4**	**3**	**2**
3	**4**	**2** (8+)	**1**	**5**

75

5 (20×)	**4** (2÷)	**2**	**3** (2−)	**1**
4	**1** (6+)	**3**	**2**	**5** (1−)
3 (120×)	**2**	**5**	**1** (30×)	**4**
1 (2−)	**3**	**4**	**5**	**2**
2 (2)	**5** (20×)	**1**	**4**	**3**

76

2 (2÷)	**4**	**3** (15×)	**1**	**5**
4 (12+)	**5** (7+)	**1**	**2** (1−)	**3**
3	**1**	**5** (5)	**4** (7+)	**2**
5	**2** (6+)	**4** (1−)	**3**	**1**
1	**3**	**2** (40×)	**5**	**4**

77

5 **5**	2÷ **1**	**2**	1− **4**	**3**
2÷ **1**	**2**	5 **5**	2− **3**	40× **4**
1− **3**	1− **5**	**4**	**1**	**2**
4	6+ **3**	**1**	**2**	**5**
2÷ **2**	**4**	9+ **3**	**5**	**1**

78

2− **3**	**5**	1− **4**	1− **1**	**2**
2÷ **2**	**4**	**5**	12+ **3**	5+ **1**
5× **1**	1− **2**	**3**	**5**	**4**
5	**1**	2÷ **2**	**4**	10+ **3**
1− **4**	**3**	**1**	**2**	**5**

79

6+ **1**	**5**	24× **4**	**3**	**2**
2÷ **2**	6+ **1**	1− **5**	**4**	2− **3**
4	**3**	2÷ **1**	**2**	**5**
12+ **5**	**2**	6+ **3**	**1**	10+ **4**
3	**4**	**2**	**5**	**1**

80

3 **3**	2÷ **4**	**2**	10× **5**	6+ **1**
1− **4**	11+ **5**	**1**	**2**	**3**
5	**1**	1− **3**	**4**	**2**
2	**3**	6+ **5**	**1**	60× **4**
1− **1**	**2**	4 **4**	**3**	**5**

81

4− **1**	**5**	40× **2**	1− **3**	**4**
12+ **3**	2÷ **2**	**4**	**1**	**5**
4	**1**	2− **3**	**5**	1− **2**
5	120× **4**	2÷ **1**	**2**	**3**
2	**3**	**5**	3− **4**	**1**

82

24× **2**	**4**	**3**	2− **1**	3− **5**
12+ **5**	7+ **1**	**4**	**3**	**2**
3	**2**	10+ **1**	**5**	**4**
4	2− **3**	**5**	2÷ **2**	**1**
6+ **1**	**5**	9+ **2**	**4**	**3**

83

6+ **2**	**1**	**3**	1− **4**	**5**
2− **5**	**3**	2÷ **4**	**2**	12× **1**
4− **1**	**5**	40× **2**	**3**	**4**
1− **3**	**4**	**5**	6× **1**	**2**
4	8+ **2**	**1**	**5**	**3**

84

6× **2**	**1**	2− **3**	**5**	2÷ **4**
12+ **5**	**3**	12× **4**	**1**	**2**
4	20× **2**	**1**	**3**	10+ **5**
3	**5**	**2**	**4**	**1**
20× **1**	**4**	**5**	1− **2**	**3**

2÷ 2	**1−** 3	4	**15×** 5	**4−** 1
4	**11+** 2	**8+** 1	3	5
2− 1	4	5	2	**12×** 3
3	5	**2÷** 2	1	4
6+ 5	1	**9+** 3	4	2

10× 2	**12+** 5	4	3	**2−** 1
5	**2÷** 1	**2−** 2	4	3
1	2	**2−** 3	**1−** 5	4
11+ 3	4	5	**2÷** 1	2
4 4	3	1	**3−** 2	5

40× 2	**60×** 3	4	5	**8+** 1
5	4	**2÷** 2	1	3
12× 3	**4−** 5	1	**2** 2	4
4	1	**2−** 5	**1−** 3	2
1− 1	2	3	**1−** 4	5

60× 4	3	1	**3−** 5	2
5	**1−** 4	**8+** 3	**1−** 2	1
6+ 1	5	2	3	**1−** 4
3	**2÷** 2	**80×** 4	1	5
2	1	5	4	**3** 3

89

$^{1-}$3	$^{1-}$4	5	$^{2÷}$2	1
2	$^{15×}$5	1	$^{1-}$4	3
$^{3-}$4	3	$^{10+}$2	$^{4-}$1	5
1	$^{10×}$2	3	5	$^{2÷}$4
5	1	$^{1-}$4	3	2

90

$^{2÷}$1	$^{1-}$4	$^{40×}$2	$^{2-}$3	5
2	3	5	4	$^{1-}$1
^{4}4	$^{10×}$5	$^{2-}$3	1	2
$^{2-}$5	1	$^{10+}$4	$^{5+}$2	3
3	2	1	5	^{4}4

91

$^{2-}$3	5	$^{1-}$1	2	$^{1-}$4
$^{9+}$1	$^{24×}$2	3	$^{1-}$4	5
2	1	4	5	$^{2-}$3
5	$^{11+}$4	$^{10×}$2	^{3}3	1
4	3	5	$^{2÷}$1	2

92

$^{2-}$2	4	$^{15×}$3	5	1
$^{13+}$3	2	^{4}4	$^{2÷}$1	$^{1-}$5
5	3	$^{6+}$1	2	4
$^{3-}$4	$^{10×}$1	5	$^{1-}$3	2
1	5	2	$^{1-}$4	3

93

1− 5	9+ 1	3	4 4	6× 2
4	12+ 3	5	2÷ 2	1
1− 2	5	4	1	3
3	2÷ 2	1	1− 5	4
7+ 1	4	2	2− 3	5

94

2÷ 1	2	20× 5	1− 4	3
1− 4	5	1	1− 3	2
10+ 5	2− 3	4	7+ 2	1
3	1	3− 2	5	4
2	4 4	9+ 3	1	5

95

3− 2	4× 1	4	11+ 5	3
5	10+ 2	1	3	3− 4
3	5	2÷ 2	4	1
12× 4	3	60× 5	2÷ 1	3− 2
1	4	3	2	5

96

2− 5	3	8+ 1	2÷ 4	2
24× 4	2	5	2− 3	1 1
3	10+ 4	2	1	2− 5
1	5	24× 4	2 2	3
2	1	3	1− 5	4

97

³3	³⁰ˣ1	5	¹⁵⁺2	4
⁸⁺1	2	3	4	5
2	⁸⁺3	4	¹⁵ˣ5	1
5	⁸⁰ˣ4	1	3	¹⁻2
4	5	²÷2	1	3

98

³⁻1	4	¹⁻2	⁶⁰ˣ3	5
³⁻2	5	3	4	¹⁰⁺1
¹⁻3	²÷2	1	5	4
4	⁹⁺3	5	1	⁶ˣ2
⁴⁻5	1	²÷4	2	3

99

²÷4	2	¹²⁰ˣ3	⁴⁻5	1
¹⁻1	¹²⁺3	2	4	5
2	1	5	3	²÷4
²⁻3	5	³⁻4	1	2
¹⁰⁺5	4	1	¹⁻2	3

100

²⁻1	3	²⁴ˣ4	¹²⁺2	5
⁸ˣ4	2	3	5	⁴⁺1
2	1	¹²⁺5	4	3
²⁻3	5	2	1	²÷4
¹⁻5	4	²⁻1	3	2

101

15× 5	**3−** 2	**2÷** 4	**2−** 3	1
3	5	2	**5+** 1	4
2÷ 2	1	**10+** 3	**9+** 4	5
3− 1	4	5	2	**1−** 3
12× 4	3	**6+** 1	5	2

102

60× 4	3	**12+** 5	2	**1** 1
5	1	2	3	**1−** 4
7+ 1	2	**12×** 4	**25×** 5	3
1− 2	4	3	1	5
3	**4−** 5	1	**2÷** 4	2

103

15× 5	3	**8+** 1	**2÷** 4	2
1− 3	5	2	**12+** 1	4
4	**2−** 1	3	2	5
4× 1	2	**17+** 4	5	**4+** 3
2	**4** 4	5	3	1

104

1− 2	3	**20×** 4	1	5
10+ 5	**2÷** 4	2	**4+** 3	1
4	**6×** 1	3	**3−** 5	2
1	2	**5** 5	**7+** 4	**1−** 3
2− 3	5	1	2	4

105

2÷ 4	8+ 5	2÷ 1	2	12× 3
2	3	2- 5	4	1
3- 1	4	3	13+ 5	2
30× 3	2	2÷ 4	1	5
5	1	2	1- 3	4

106

11+ 1	3	2	1- 5	4
12× 3	5	3- 1	4	1- 2
4	1	3- 5	2	3
3- 5	2÷ 2	1- 4	3	1 1
2	4	3 3	6+ 1	5

107

40× 4	2- 1	3	2 2	8+ 5
5	7+ 2	4	1	3
2	6+ 5	1	1- 3	4
2- 1	3	16+ 5	4	2÷ 2
1- 3	4	2	5	1

108

12× 4	3- 2	9+ 5	3	8+ 1
3	5	1- 4	1	2
1	20× 4	3	2÷ 2	5
5	1	8+ 2	4	1- 3
2	3	1	5 5	4

109

3− 5	45× 3	5+ 1	4	9+ 2
2	1	1− 5	3	4
3	5	4	2÷ 2	14+ 1
9+ 4	12× 2	3	1	5
1	4	2	5	3

110

2÷ 4	2	6+ 1	2− 3	5
1− 2	3	5	12× 4	1
4− 5	2÷ 4	2	1	3
1	2− 5	3	3− 2	2÷ 4
8+ 3	1	4	5	2

111

40× 4	10+ 3	5	1 1	2÷ 2
5	2	10+ 4	7+ 3	1
2	5	1	4	60× 3
2− 3	2÷ 1	2	10× 5	4
1	7+ 4	3	2	5

112

1− 4	5	2− 3	1	2− 2
2− 1	3	1− 5	10+ 2	4
10+ 2	8× 1	4	3	5
3	4	2÷ 2	20× 5	1
5	2	1	4	3 3

113

9+ 1	**40×** 5	2	**3** 3	**3−** 4
3	**1−** 2	4	**11+** 5	1
5	3	**6+** 1	4	2
2÷ 4	**3−** 1	5	**10+** 2	3
2	4	**4+** 3	1	5

114

14+ 3	**3−** 4	1	**10×** 2	5
1	5	**10+** 3	**2÷** 4	2
5	2	4	**2−** 3	**4+** 1
24× 4	1	**3−** 2	5	3
2	3	5	**3−** 1	4

115

12× 3	1	4	**3−** 2	**9+** 5
2÷ 1	2	**9+** 3	5	4
1− 4	3	5	**10+** 1	2
12+ 2	5	1	4	3
5	**9+** 4	2	3	**1** 1

116

2÷ 1	**75×** 5	3	**1−** 4	**2÷** 2
2	**1** 1	5	3	4
2− 4	2	**8+** 1	**5** 5	**2−** 3
2− 3	**1−** 4	2	1	5
5	3	4	**1−** 2	1

117

5+ 1	**1−** 4	**10×** 2	5	**1−** 3
4	5	**2−** 1	3	2
10+ 5	2	3	**3−** 4	1
5+ 3	**4−** 1	5	**2÷** 2	**1−** 4
2	**1−** 3	4	1	5

118

4− 1	**3−** 4	**30×** 2	5	3
5	1	**1−** 4	3	**11+** 2
11+ 2	**2−** 3	1	4	5
3	2	**20×** 5	1	4
4	**2−** 5	3	**2÷** 2	1

119

2÷ 1	2	**1−** 4	**4+** 3	**10×** 5
1− 4	5	3	1	2
2− 5	3	**80×** 2	4	1
1− 3	**3−** 1	5	2	**12×** 4
2	4	**4−** 1	5	3

120

1− 2	**7+** 1	4	**20×** 5	**2−** 3
3	2	1	4	5
5+ 1	4	**2−** 5	3	**8×** 2
1− 5	**2−** 3	**1−** 2	1	4
4	5	3	**2÷** 2	1

121

30× 2	3	5	**⁴** 4	**2÷** 1
1− 4	**6+** 1	**2−** 3	5	2
3	5	**¹** 1	**7+** 2	**1−** 4
6+ 1	**2−** 4	2	3	5
5	2	**3−** 4	1	**³** 3

122

40× 5	4	**2÷** 1	2	**2−** 3
1	2	**1−** 3	**7+** 4	5
2÷ 4	**2−** 5	2	3	**4×** 1
2	3	**1−** 5	1	4
2− 3	1	4	**3−** 5	2

123

20× 5	4	**2÷** 2	1	**2−** 3
8+ 4	3	**17+** 5	**8+** 2	1
1	5	3	4	2
2÷ 2	1	4	**2−** 3	5
6× 3	2	1	**20×** 5	4

124

2− 5	3	**20×** 1	**2÷** 2	4
6+ 3	2	5	4	1
1	**13+** 4	2	3	**2−** 5
11+ 2	**¹** 1	4	**9+** 5	3
4	5	3	1	**²** 2

125

11+ 3	4	10× 2	5	2÷ 1
3− 5	1	3	3− 4	2
2	15× 3	5	1	1− 4
1− 4	5	7+ 1	2	3
2÷ 1	2	4	2− 3	5

126

5+ 4	1	2÷ 2	60× 3	5
1− 3	11+ 2	1	11+ 5	4
2	4	5	1	1− 3
4− 1	5	11+ 3	4	2
5	3 3	4	1− 2	1

127

60× 3	2÷ 2	3− 5	6+ 1	4
5	4	2	90× 3	1
4	15× 3	20× 1	2	5
1− 2	1	4	5	3
1	5	3 3	2− 4	2

128

5+ 4	1	2− 3	4− 5	40× 2
6× 2	3	5	1	4
2÷ 1	2	2− 4	12× 3	5
2− 3	20× 5	2	4	4+ 1
5	4	2÷ 1	2	3

129

¹⁻ 4	²⁻ 1	²÷ 2	²⁻ 5	3
5	3	4	⁶⁺ 2	1
⁶ˣ 2	⁶⁺ 5	1	3	²÷ 4
3	²⁻ 4	²⁻ 5	¹ 1	2
1	2	3	¹⁻ 4	5

130

⁴⁺ 3	1	¹⁻ 2	¹⁻ 5	4
²÷ 2	¹⁻ 4	3	¹⁻ 1	²⁻ 5
4	5	³⁻ 1	2	3
¹⁰ˣ 5	2	4	²⁻ 3	1
1	²⁻ 3	5	²⁻ 4	2

131

²⁰ˣ 4	⁷⁺ 2	5	²⁻ 3	1
1	5	¹⁻ 3	4	¹⁶ˣ 2
²⁻ 5	3	⁵⁺ 1	2	4
²÷ 2	1	4	⁸⁺ 5	¹⁵ˣ 3
¹⁻ 3	4	2	1	5

132

¹²ˣ 3	2	⁶⁺ 1	⁷⁺ 5	⁷⁺ 4
1	¹⁻ 4	5	2	3
2	3	²÷ 4	⁴⁻ 1	5
¹⁻ 4	5	2	¹⁻ 3	²÷ 1
⁴⁻ 5	1	³ 3	4	2

133

12× 3	1− 2	4− 5	1	2− 4
1	3	2÷ 4	9+ 5	2
4	10+ 5	2	3	1
7+ 2	1	2− 3	9+ 4	5
5	4	1	1− 2	3

134

24× 4	30× 2	3	6+ 1	5 5
3	5	1	4	2÷ 2
2	8+ 3	1− 4	5	1
1	4	10+ 5	2	1− 3
10× 5	1	2	3	4

135

2 2	20× 1	4	5	2− 3
1− 4	3	2÷ 1	2	5
1− 1	2	12+ 5	3	5+ 4
2− 3	11+ 5	2	4	1
5	4	2− 3	1	2 2

136

9+ 2	20× 5	4	8+ 1	3 3
3	4	4− 1	5	2
1− 4	6× 3	5	2÷ 2	1
5	1	2	10+ 3	1− 4
2÷ 1	2	3	4	5

137

40× 4	1	**2−** 3	**3−** 2	5
2	5	1	**12+** 3	4
9+ 1	**7+** 3	4	5	**2÷** 2
3	**3−** 2	5	**8+** 4	1
5	**2÷** 4	2	1	3

138

1− 4	**6×** 3	2	**8+** 1	**3−** 5
5	**10×** 1	4	3	2
2	5	**2−** 1	**11+** 4	3
2÷ 1	2	3	**8+** 5	4
12+ 3	4	5	2	1

139

2÷ 4	2	**10+** 1	3	5
2− 5	**3** 3	**40×** 2	1	**10+** 4
3	4	5	2	1
2÷ 2	1	**1−** 4	5	3
4− 1	5	**9+** 3	4	2

140

6+ 3	1	**40×** 4	5	2
2÷ 1	2	**2−** 3	**1−** 4	**4−** 5
2	**60×** 4	5	3	1
5	3	**12+** 1	**2−** 2	4
4	5	2	**2−** 1	3

141

⁵⁺ 1	4	¹⁻ 2	3	¹²⁰ˣ 5
⁴⁻ 5	1	⁷⁺ 4	2	3
²⁻ 3	5	1	4	2
²÷ 4	¹⁰⁺ 2	¹⁵ˣ 3	5	1
2	3	5	³⁻ 1	4

142

³⁻ 4	²⁰ˣ 5	²⁻ 1	⁵⁺ 3	2
1	4	3	³⁰ˣ 2	5
²⁻ 5	²÷ 2	⁴⁰ˣ 4	1	3
3	1	2	5	⁵⁺ 4
¹⁻ 2	3	¹⁻ 5	4	1

143

³ 3	²⁰ˣ 1	¹⁻ 4	³⁻ 2	5
4	5	3	⁴⁻ 1	²⁻ 2
³⁻ 2	⁷⁺ 3	¹⁻ 1	5	4
5	4	2	²⁻ 3	1
²÷ 1	2	⁵ 5	¹⁻ 4	3

144

⁶ˣ 3	2	1	¹⁻ 5	4
¹⁻ 4	5	²⁻ 2	⁷⁺ 1	3
⁹⁺ 5	3	4	2	1
²÷ 2	1	¹⁰⁺ 3	4	³⁻ 5
1	¹⁻ 4	5	3	2

145

100× 1	4	5	1− 3	2
1− 3	5	3− 1	2÷ 2	1− 4
2	1− 3	4	1	5
1− 4	2	6+ 3	6+ 5	1
5	1	2	1− 4	3

146

4− 1	5	120× 2	3	4
5+ 4	1	5	2÷ 2	2− 3
2− 3	11+ 2	3− 1	4	5
5	3	4	1− 1	2
2	4	9+ 3	5	1

147

4 4	10× 5	1	2	3
1	2	1− 3	4	7+ 5
2− 5	3	3− 4	1	2
2− 3	1	40× 2	5	4
2÷ 2	4	9+ 5	3	1

148

3− 4	24× 3	2	9+ 1	5
1	4	3− 5	2	3
2− 3	10× 5	1	2÷ 4	2
5	2	1− 4	3	3− 1
1− 2	1	2− 3	5	4

149

²⁻3	5	²÷2	³⁻1	4
²⁻2	¹1	4	²⁻3	5
4	¹⁻3	²⁻1	³⁻5	2
¹⁰ˣ5	4	3	¹¹⁺2	²⁻1
1	2	5	4	3

150

¹⁻5	4	²÷1	2	¹⁻3
¹⁰⁺4	1	3	²⁰ˣ5	2
²⁻3	5	2	1	4
⁶⁺1	⁹⁺2	4	3	⁶⁺5
2	3	¹⁻5	4	1

151

¹⁵⁺7	5	³⁶ˣ2	3	6	⁶⁺1	4
3	¹³⁺7	6	¹⁴⁰ˣ4	⁷⁺2	5	1
²÷4	²⁴ˣ1	5	7	¹⁵¹²ˣ3	6	2
2	6	²⁻3	5	⁶⁻1	⁷⁺4	7
¹⁴⁺5	4	²ˣ1	2	7	3	6
6	⁴⁻3	7	1	²⁻4	2	¹⁰⁵ˣ5
1	2	¹⁵⁺4	6	5	7	3

152

⁹⁺5	⁸⁴ˣ3	4	7	⁷⁺6	1	⁷⁺2
3	¹⁻6	7	⁴⁰ˣ4	2	5	1
1	²÷2	²⁻5	¹²⁺3	7	¹³⁺6	4
⁶⁷²ˣ4	1	3	2	²⁵ˣ5	7	³⁶ˣ6
7	4	6	5	1	2	3
⁶⁰ˣ2	⁶⁻7	1	¹³⁺6	4	3	¹⁶⁺5
6	5	⁶⁺2	1	3	4	7

153

2÷ 6	3	100× 5	672× 4	2	7	15+ 1
6− 7	5	1	3	4	6	2
1	4	840× 7	5	3	2	6
5− 2	7	4	¹ 1	90× 6	5	3
240× 5	2	13+ 6	7	15× 1	3	12+ 4
4	6	18× 3	3÷ 2	5	1	7
3	1	2	6	16+ 7	4	5

154

5− 2	5	1− 3	180× 7	13+ 6	4× 4	1
7	4	5	6	2	1	16+ 3
15× 5	6− 1	7	168× 2	3	6	4
1	² 2	17+ 4	3	7	30× 5	6
3	7	6	4	3+ 1	2	3− 5
2− 6	2÷ 3	8+ 1	5	10+ 4	147× 7	2
4	6	2	1	5	3	7

155

17+ 7	2	12+ 3	4	5	13+ 6	1
2	12+ 5	6	15× 3	49× 1	7	4
6	2÷ 3	1	5	7	2÷ 4	2
3− 1	6	70× 5	6− 7	⁴ 4	2	90× 3
4	7	2	1	2÷ 6	3	5
2− 5	16× 4	12+ 7	2	3	70× 1	6
3	1	4	⁶ 6	2	5	7

156

3÷ 2	28× 7	1	4	8+ 5	3	1− 6
6	80× 4	12+ 7	3	2	36× 1	5
5	1	4	⁷ 7	6	2	3
3÷ 3	1− 6	5	12× 2	5+ 1	4	140× 7
1	² 2	2÷ 3	6	4− 7	5	4
11+ 4	2− 5	6	1	3	1− 7	2÷ 2
7	3	40× 2	5	4	6	1

157

7+ **4**	12+ **3**	**2**	**7**	12× **6**	**1**	4− **5**
3	168× **6**	3− **7**	**4**	**2**	100× **5**	**1**
7	**1**	3− **3**	**6**	**5**	**4**	56× **2**
3÷ **2**	**4**	5 **5**	9× **3**	**1**	16+ **6**	**7**
6	3− **5**	3+ **1**	**2**	**3**	**7**	**4**
6+ **1**	**2**	9+ **4**	**5**	13+ **7**	**3**	2÷ **6**
5	42× **7**	**6**	**1**	**4**	**2**	**3**

158

17+ **6**	**5**	**3**	6− **1**	**7**	2÷ **2**	**4**
3	84× **2**	**6**	**7**	20× **4**	**1**	**5**
16× **4**	**1**	21× **7**	**3**	14+ **6**	16+ **5**	2÷ **2**
42× **2**	**4**	1− **5**	**6**	**3**	**7**	**1**
7	**3**	3+ **1**	**2**	**5**	**4**	16+ **6**
12+ **5**	7 **7**	2÷ **2**	**4**	**1**	**6**	**3**
1	**6**	4 **4**	10× **5**	**2**	4− **3**	**7**

159

2− **5**	2÷ **2**	2÷ **3**	**6**	6− **1**	**7**	2− **4**
7	**1**	15× **5**	**3**	15+ **2**	**4**	**6**
3+ **2**	10+ **7**	56× **4**	**1**	210× **6**	**3**	30× **5**
1	**3**	**7**	4 **4**	**5**	**6**	**2**
2− **6**	**4**	**2**	210× **5**	**7**	3+ **1**	**3**
1− **4**	**5**	**6**	**7**	3 **3**	**2**	8+ **1**
3	**6**	1− **1**	**2**	9+ **4**	**5**	**7**

160

6− **7**	18× **3**	28× **4**	3÷ **2**	**6**	3+ **1**	60× **5**
1	**6**	**7**	9+ **4**	**5**	**2**	**3**
16+ **5**	**1**	60× **2**	2÷ **3**	42× **7**	**6**	**4**
3	**4**	**5**	**6**	10+ **1**	**7**	**2**
4	14+ **7**	**6**	20× **5**	**2**	1− **3**	8+ **1**
3÷ **6**	**2**	3÷ **3**	**1**	**4**	15+ **5**	**7**
2	**5**	**1**	4− **7**	**3**	**4**	**6**

161

15× 3	5	**2÷** 2	4	**6−** 1	7	**72×** 6
6× 6	1	**4−** 7	3	**7+** 5	2	4
1	**14+** 2	5	7	**11+** 6	**60×** 4	3
3− 7	4	**6** 6	**3+** 2	3	5	**6−** 1
60× 5	**24×** 6	4	1	2	3	7
4	3	**4−** 1	5	**1−** 7	6	**3−** 2
9+ 2	7	**2÷** 3	6	**3−** 4	1	5

162

1− 3	4	**840×** 6	**4−** 1	5	**14×** 2	7
3+ 2	1	5	7	4	**2÷** 6	3
3− 4	7	**144×** 3	2	1	**150×** 5	6
1	**84×** 2	4	3	6	**6−** 7	5
1− 5	6	7	4	**84×** 3	1	**3+** 2
6	**6×** 3	2	**14+** 5	7	4	1
12+ 7	5	1	6	2	**7+** 3	4

163

6× 6	1	**11+** 4	**9+** 5	7	**30×** 2	3
1	**5+** 2	7	4	6	**4−** 3	5
2− 5	3	**6×** 1	**14×** 2	**3−** 4	7	**4−** 6
3	**20×** 5	6	7	1	**2−** 4	2
11+ 7	4	**3−** 5	**9×** 3	**2** 2	6	**6−** 1
4	**15+** 6	2	1	3	**15+** 5	7
2	7	**2÷** 3	6	5	1	4

164

3÷ 3	1	**15+** 4	**3÷** 2	**13+** 7	6	**15×** 5
1− 5	4	1	6	**14×** 2	7	3
1− 1	3	7	**11+** 4	5	2	**11+** 6
2	**35×** 7	5	1	**504×** 6	**3** 3	4
6 6	**180×** 5	2	7	3	4	1
2÷ 4	2	6	**2−** 3	**20×** 1	5	**9+** 7
42× 7	6	3	5	4	1	2

165

¹⁻ 5	4	⁴⁻ 3	³÷ 2	6	⁷ˣ 1	7
²÷ 3	6	7	³⁻ 5	2	³⁻ 4	1
²÷ 2	⁴⁻ 1	5	¹⁶⁸ˣ 6	⁸⁺ 4	7	¹⁴⁺ 3
4	³ 3	¹³⁺ 2	7	1	5	6
²⁻ 7	5	1	4	3	²÷ 6	⁸⁰ˣ 2
⁴⁻ 6	2	4	⁶⁻ 1	7	3	5
⁶⁻ 1	7	6	²⁻ 3	5	2	4

166

¹⁻ 5	²÷ 1	¹⁸⁺ 6	2	3	¹⁻ 7	⁷⁺ 4
4	2	5	⁶⁻ 7	1	6	3
³⁻ 7	4	2	²⁵ˣ 1	5	²÷ 3	6
¹⁰⁺ 1	⁸⁴ˣ 3	4	5	¹²⁺ 6	2	⁷⁰ˣ 7
6	7	⁶⁻ 1	³ 3	¹³⁺ 2	4	5
3	¹³⁺ 5	7	²⁴ˣ 6	4	⁵ˣ 1	2
2	6	³ 3	4	7	5	1

167

⁴ˣ 2	1	⁴⁻ 3	¹³⁺ 7	⁴⁸⁰ˣ 5	6	4
⁴⁻ 3	2	7	6	1	4	¹⁵ˣ 5
7	²⁻ 4	6	¹²⁺ 1	2	5	3
¹⁵ˣ 1	3	5	4	⁸⁴ˣ 7	2	6
¹⁻ 6	5	⁹⁺ 4	2	3	⁶⁻ 7	1
¹⁻ 4	¹³⁺ 7	²÷ 1	²⁻ 5	¹³⁺ 6	3	⁹⁺ 2
5	6	2	3	4	¹ 1	7

168

¹²⁰ˣ 4	3	³÷ 2	¹³⁺ 6	7	⁴⁻ 5	1
5	1	6	³⁵ˣ 7	²¹⁶ˣ 3	⁴ 4	⁴⁻ 2
2	¹⁰⁵ˣ 5	7	1	4	3	6
²÷ 1	2	3	5	6	²⁰⁺ 7	4
²÷ 3	6	¹³⁺ 5	4	1	2	7
²⁰⁺ 7	¹⁶ˣ 4	1	3	¹²⁰ˣ 2	6	¹⁵ˣ 5
6	7	4	2	5	1	3

169

2÷ **4**	12+ **5**	1− **2**	20× **1**	13+ **6**	**7**	15× **3**
2	**7**	**3**	**4**	**1**	11+ **6**	**5**
3÷ **3**	1− **2**	168× **6**	**5**	**4**	**1**	1− **7**
1	**3**	**4**	9+ **2**	**7**	60× **5**	**6**
1− **5**	**4**	**7**	126× **6**	**2**	**3**	1 **1**
1− **6**	6× **1**	15× **5**	**7**	**3**	**2**	2÷ **4**
7	**6**	**1**	**3**	1− **5**	**4**	**2**

170

2÷ **3**	210× **7**	**6**	**5**	3+ **2**	**1**	3− **4**
6	3+ **2**	20× **5**	**4**	**1**	2− **3**	**7**
2− **4**	**1**	126× **3**	**7**	**6**	**5**	3− **2**
2	1− **4**	**7**	3÷ **1**	**3**	1− **6**	**5**
6− **1**	**3**	**4**	3− **2**	**5**	**7**	2÷ **6**
7	150× **5**	2÷ **1**	2÷ **6**	3− **4**	2− **2**	**3**
5	**6**	**2**	**3**	**7**	**4**	1 **1**

171

6− **7**	**1**	18+ **2**	**3**	**6**	1− **4**	**5**
18× **3**	1− **7**	**6**	4 **4**	**2**	**5**	6+ **1**
2	**3**	2− **5**	13+ **6**	**7**	**1**	**4**
20× **4**	2÷ **2**	**3**	2× **1**	14+ **5**	**6**	13+ **7**
5	**4**	196× **7**	**2**	**1**	**3**	**6**
12+ **6**	**5**	**1**	**7**	**4**	12× **2**	**3**
1	10+ **6**	**4**	15+ **5**	**3**	**7**	**2**

172

12+ **2**	**3**	4− **1**	**5**	13+ **7**	**6**	16× **4**
42× **7**	**2**	**5**	2÷ **6**	**3**	**4**	**1**
6	1− **4**	336× **7**	1− **1**	17+ **2**	2− **3**	**5**
60× **1**	**5**	**4**	**2**	**6**	4− **7**	**3**
3	6 **6**	**2**	**4**	**5**	6− **1**	**7**
4	6− **7**	**6**	2− **3**	**1**	60× **5**	**2**
5	**1**	4− **3**	**7**	2÷ **4**	**2**	**6**

173

16+ 1	3	14+ 5	42× 7	2: 2	4	2− 6
5	4	2	6	6− 1	7	3: 3
3	19+ 6	7	10× 2	5	4× 1	4
4	2	2− 3	5	1− 7	6	1
3÷ 6	7	24× 4	3÷ 1	3	14+ 5	14× 2
2	13+ 5	1	1− 4	6	3	7
7	1	6	3	40× 4	2	5

174

3− 6	4− 1	5	24× 4	1− 2	3	2− 7
3	5− 2	7	6	3− 4	1	5
6− 7	2− 4	6	1	8+ 3	5	2÷ 2
1	3: 3	5− 2	7	1− 5	6	4
175× 5	7	3+ 1	2	14+ 6	84× 4	3
2÷ 2	5	4	3	1	7	5− 6
4	1260× 6	3	5	7	2	1

175

6− 1	7	1440× 3	5	3÷ 2	6	2− 4
2520× 5	5− 6	4	14+ 7	1	3	2
3	1	6	4	16+ 7	2	35× 5
4	15+ 2	5	3: 3	6	1	7
6	5	28× 7	2	3	14+ 4	1
7	3	2	1	4	5	21+ 6
6+ 2	4	7+ 1	6	5	7	3

176

13+ 6	7	12+ 4	3	5	1− 1	2
2− 4	6	15+ 3	7	1	10× 2	5
30× 3	6× 1	6	4	13+ 2	5	11+ 7
2	2− 4	1	11+ 5	6	11+ 7	3
5	2	70× 7	6	4− 3	4	1
6− 1	8+ 3	5	2	7	3− 6	24× 4
7	5	2÷ 2	1	4: 4	3	6

177

²10×	⁴8+	⁵8+	3	⁷14+	1	6
5	3	²12×	⁷28×	4	⁶1−	¹3−
⁶2÷	1	3	2	⁵5	7	4
3	⁵20×	4	⁶36×	1	²5−	7
⁴3−	7	¹4−	5	6	³2−	²1−
¹6−	⁶3÷	⁷1−	⁴8×	2	5	3
7	2	6	1	³60×	4	5

178

⁶13+	⁵420×	7	¹5−	⁴2÷	2	³1−
7	4	¹20+	6	5	³72×	2
3	1	2	5	7	6	4
²1−	⁷28×	4	³2÷	6	¹1	⁵35×
1	²48×	6	4	³15×	5	7
⁵1−	6	³42×	7	2	⁴5+	1
⁴12+	3	5	²2÷	1	7	⁶1−

179

⁶19+	4	3	¹294×	7	²3−	5
³36×	²3+	6	7	⁴21+	5	1
4	1	2	3	5	6	⁷294×
1	3	⁴14+	5	⁶6	7	2
⁷70×	⁶1−	5	²36×	1	⁴9+	3
2	5	⁷49×	6	3	1	4
5	7	1	⁴2÷	2	³2÷	6

180

³5+	2	⁴1−	⁷12+	5	¹6×	6
²9+	6	5	³1−	⁴11+	7	1
1	³1−	2	4	7	6	⁵105×
⁵12+	⁴1−	3	¹8+	⁶3÷	2	7
7	¹7+	6	5	²1−	⁴1−	3
⁶13+	7	¹6−	2	3	5	⁴24×
⁴20×	5	7	⁶5−	1	3	2

181

25× 5	6 6	49× 1	7	12+ 2	12+ 3	4
1	5	7	4	6	2	3
1− 3	2	18+ 5	6	7	3− 4	1
2÷ 2	1	3÷ 6	9+ 3	3− 4	2− 7	5
17+ 4	1008× 3	2	5	1	1− 6	15+ 7
6	7	4	1	9+ 3	5	2
7	4	3	² 2	5	1	6

182

2− 5	3	13+ 4	10+ 2	2− 6	6− 1	7
2÷ 3	2÷ 2	7	5	4	1− 6	4− 1
6	4	2	3	¹ 1	7	5
7× 1	7	14+ 5	6	3	240× 4	2
2 2	1	1008× 3	4	7	5	6
3− 7	11+ 5	6	7× 1	2	10+ 3	1− 4
4	6	1	7	5	2	3

183

30× 6	1	80× 4	5	504× 3	7	2
6− 1	5	13+ 7	4	6	2	14+ 3
7	12× 3	6	3+ 1	2	60× 4	5
2 2	4	11+ 1	3	7	5	6
2− 5	1− 6	7+ 2	3− 7	4	3	12+ 1
3	7	5	11+ 2	30× 1	6	4
2÷ 4	2	3	6	5	1	7

184

2÷ 1	1− 5	4	11+ 3	2	6	4− 7
2	42× 7	120× 6	4	5	4× 1	3
3	2	6− 5	3− 5	1− 6	4	1
168× 4	2÷ 6	1	2	7	1− 3	120× 5
7	3	3− 5	1	1− 4	2	6
6	20× 1	2	7	3	14+ 5	4
5	4	10+ 3	6	1	7	2

185

³ˣ3	1	¹¹⁺4	5	2	²⁵²ˣ7	6
1	²⁻5	7	³⁻4	6	2	¹³⁺3
¹¹⁺4	3	¹⁰⁺6	1	7	5	¹³⁺2
³⁻2	4	1	3	²⁰ˣ5	6	⁸⁺7
5	¹⁻6	¹⁴ˣ2	7	4	³÷3	1
¹⁵⁺6	7	¹⁴⁺5	⁶⁺2	3	1	⁸⁰ˣ4
7	2	3	6	1	4	5

186

⁵⁻6	1	⁸⁴⁰ˣ7	5	4	⁵⁺3	2
¹⁰⁵ˣ7	3	5	6	³÷1	¹²⁺2	4
⁹⁺4	¹⁴⁺2	¹1	⁶⁻7	3	6	¹⁴⁺5
2	5	²÷4	1	⁶6	⁶⁻7	3
3	7	2	²÷4	²⁻5	1	6
¹⁴⁺5	6	3	2	7	³⁻4	1
³⁻1	4	¹¹⁺6	3	2	²⁻5	7

187

⁵⁴ˣ6	3	⁵⁶ˣ4	2	7	²⁰ˣ1	5
3	⁶6	¹⁴⁺7	5	2	4	1
³⁺2	²÷4	¹⁸⁺3	1	5	¹³⁺6	⁴⁻7
1	2	5	¹⁻6	4	7	3
⁶⁺5	1	⁹⁺6	7	²÷3	²⁻2	4
²⁻7	5	1	¹²ˣ4	6	¹⁻3	2
³⁻4	7	2	3	1	¹⁻5	6

188

¹²ˣ1	4	¹³⁺5	2	6	¹⁶⁺3	7
3	¹²⁺5	4	³⁺1	2	⁷7	6
²÷2	1	3	¹⁻5	⁷7	²⁻6	4
¹⁴⁺5	¹⁶⁺3	7	6	¹⁶ˣ1	4	¹⁰ˣ2
7	2	6	¹⁵⁺3	4	5	1
¹⁶⁺4	6	²2	7	5	⁹⁺1	3
6	⁶⁻7	1	⁹⁺4	3	2	5

189

7 ⁶⁻	4 ³⁶⁰ˣ	5	1	3	6	2 ¹²⁺
1	7 ¹³⁺	6	4 ¹¹²ˣ	5	2	3
3 ⁷⁺	2	4	7	1	5 ¹⁵⁺	6
2	1 ¹²ˣ	3 ¹⁸⁰ˣ	5	6 ¹⁻	7 ¹³⁺	4
4	3	2	6	7	1	5
6 ¹⁵⁰ˣ	5	7 ⁶⁻	2 ¹⁻	4 ¹⁷⁺	3 ³÷	1
5	6 ⁶	1	3	2	4	7

190

7 ²⁻	3 ⁴⁻	1 ¹³⁺	6	2 ³⁻	5	4 ²÷
5	7	6	3 ¹³⁺	4	1 ²⁻	2
2 ²÷	4	7 ⁴⁹ˣ	1	6	3	5 ¹⁵⁺
1 ⁶ˣ	6	2 ²	7	5 ²⁰ˣ	4	3
6 ¹⁻	5	3 ²⁴ˣ	4	1 ²⁻	2 ⁹⁺	7
4 ¹²ˣ	1 ¹⁻	5 ¹⁴⁺	2	3	7	6 ⁷⁺
3	2	4	5	7 ¹³⁺	6	1

191

7 ¹²⁺	1 ³⁶ˣ	6	3 ⁶ˣ	2	4 ¹⁻	5
5	6	7 ⁸⁺	1	4 ³⁻	2 ¹¹⁺	3
4 ¹⁻	3	5 ²⁻	6 ¹⁶⁸ˣ	1	7 ¹⁵⁺	2
1 ²÷	2	3	7	6 ⁶	5	4
6 ¹³⁺	7	2 ¹⁶ˣ	4	5 ¹²⁺	3	1 ⁶ˣ
3 ¹⁻	5 ¹⁰⁺	4	2	7	1	6
2	4	1	5 ²⁻	3	6 ¹⁻	7

192

4 ¹⁴⁺	7	3	2 ³⁺	1	5 ¹⁻	6
5 ²⁻	4 ⁴⁸ˣ	6 ³⁶ˣ	3	2	7 ⁵⁻	1 ⁶⁺
7	3	4	1 ³⁶ˣ	6	2	5
2 ¹⁻	5 ¹²⁺	7	6	3 ²⁻	1	4 ²÷
3	6 ²³⁺	1	7	5	4	2
1 ³⁺	2	5 ³⁻	4 ¹⁻	7	6 ²÷	3
6 ⁵⁻	1	2	5	4	3 ⁴⁻	7

193

⁷⁺ 2	3	¹⁻ 5	6	¹²⁺ 4	7	1
¹²ˣ 3	2	²÷ 6	³⁵ˣ 7	⁴⁻ 1	5	¹³⁺ 4
1	4	3	5	¹¹⁺ 6	2	7
¹⁴⁰ˣ 5	⁶⁻ 7	¹⁻ 4	3	2	³⁶ˣ 1	6
4	1	⁶⁻ 7	²÷ 2	3	6	³⁻ 5
7	¹⁸⁰ˣ 6	1	4	²⁻ 5	3	2
6	5	¹⁻ 2	1	⁷ 7	¹⁻ 4	3

194

⁶⁰ˣ 2	5	¹³⁺ 6	7	³÷ 3	1	¹²⁰ˣ 4
6	³⁻ 4	7	³÷ 3	1	2	5
²²⁺ 5	6	4	²÷ 1	2	3	⁵⁰⁴ˣ 7
1	³ 3	2	²⁻ 5	7	4	6
4	⁶⁻ 7	1	³⁻ 2	5	⁶⁰ˣ 6	3
²¹ˣ 7	¹⁻ 2	3	¹⁰⁰⁸ˣ 6	4	5	1
3	1	⁹⁺ 5	4	6	7	2

195

⁷ 7	³÷ 3	1	¹³⁺ 6	2	5	¹¹⁺ 4
⁴³²ˣ 3	6	³⁻ 4	7	¹⁴ˣ 1	2	5
6	4	¹⁵ˣ 3	1	5	7	2
⁷ˣ 1	7	⁷⁺ 5	2	¹⁻ 3	4	¹⁷⁺ 6
¹¹⁺ 2	1	²⁻ 7	5	⁴ 4	³⁶ˣ 6	3
4	5	¹⁻ 2	3	6	1	7
⁶⁰ˣ 5	2	6	¹⁴⁺ 4	7	3	1

196

²¹⁰ˣ 7	5	6	⁹⁺ 4	²÷ 1	2	¹³⁺ 3
³÷ 1	⁹⁺ 2	7	5	²÷ 6	3	4
3	⁶⁻ 1	²²⁺ 2	7	5	²⁴ˣ 4	6
²÷ 4	7	5	⁷⁺ 1	3	6	⁵⁻ 2
2	⁷⁺ 3	1	6	¹⁸⁺ 4	5	7
⁷²⁰ˣ 6	4	3	2	7	³⁵ˣ 1	5
5	6	⁹⁺ 4	3	2	7	1

197

7 ¹⁸⁺	**1** ⁹ˣ	**3**	**5** ²⁻	**2** ¹⁶⁺	**6**	**4**
2	**3**	**1** ¹	**7**	**5** ¹⁰⁺	**4**	**6** ¹⁻
3	**6**	**4** ²⁻	**2** ¹⁻	**1**	**5** ¹⁷⁵ˣ	**7**
1 ²÷	**2**	**6**	**3**	**4**	**7**	**5**
6 ¹⁸⁺	**7**	**5**	**4** ²⁻	**3** ¹⁻	**2**	**1** ¹
4 ¹³⁺	**5** ³⁻	**2**	**6**	**7** ⁶⁻	**1**	**3** ⁸⁺
5	**4**	**7** ¹⁴⁺	**1**	**6**	**3**	**2**

198

2 ³⁻	**5**	**6** ⁷²ˣ	**4**	**3**	**7** ⁸⁺	**1**
4 ¹⁴⁰ˣ	**6** ⁹⁰ˣ	**5**	**3**	**1** ¹⁻	**2**	**7** ⁵⁰⁴ˣ
1	**7**	**2** ⁶⁰ˣ	**5**	**6**	**4**	**3**
5	**2** ²÷	**3** ⁸⁴ˣ	**7**	**4**	**1** ¹¹⁺	**6**
3 ³⁷⁸ˣ	**1**	**7** ²⁸ˣ	**2** ³÷	**5** ³⁰ˣ	**6**	**4**
7	**4**	**1**	**6**	**2**	**3**	**5** ¹²⁺
6	**3**	**4** ²⁸ˣ	**1**	**7**	**5**	**2**

199

2 ¹⁷⁺	**6** ²⁶⁺	**4**	**3**	**5** ⁴⁻	**7** ²¹ˣ	**1**
5	**4**	**7**	**6**	**1**	**2** ⁶⁺	**3**
4	**2**	**6** ¹³⁺	**7** ¹⁸⁺	**3**	**1**	**5** ¹⁴⁺
1 ⁶⁻	**5** ¹⁵⁺	**2**	**4**	**6**	**3** ³	**7**
7	**3**	**5**	**1**	**4** ⁹⁶ˣ	**6**	**2**
3 ²÷	**7**	**1** ⁴²⁰ˣ	**5**	**2**	**4**	**6** ¹²⁰ˣ
6	**1**	**3**	**2**	**7**	**5**	**4**

200

6 ¹⁸⁺	**5**	**4** ⁵⁺	**1**	**2** ¹⁰ˣ	**3** ³	**7** ⁶⁻
4	**3**	**7** ¹⁶⁺	**6**	**5**	**2** ³÷	**1**
2 ⁶⁺	**1** ¹¹⁺	**3**	**4** ³⁻	**7**	**6**	**5** ¹¹⁺
3	**4**	**6** ¹⁻	**5**	**1** ¹	**7** ¹⁷⁺	**2**
1	**6**	**2** ⁴ˣ	**7** ⁴⁻	**3**	**5**	**4**
5 ²¹⁺	**7**	**1**	**2**	**6** ²⁻	**4**	**3** ²÷
7	**2**	**5** ²⁻	**3**	**4**	**1**	**6**

201

¹⁻4	⁴⁻3	³÷2	¹⁸⁺5	7	6	⁵⁺1
5	7	6	¹⁻3	³÷2	⁸⁺1	4
⁵⁶⁰ˣ2	1	5	4	6	7	¹²⁶ˣ3
³÷3	⁴4	7	¹⁰ˣ1	5	2	6
1	2	4	⁴⁻6	⁶⁰ˣ3	5	7
¹³⁺7	¹⁻6	¹⁸⁺3	2	1	4	³⁻5
6	5	1	7	4	3	2

202

⁶⁻7	²¹⁶ˣ3	6	¹⁻2	1	¹³⁺4	³⁰ˣ5
1	4	3	⁶⁺5	7	2	6
¹⁵⁺6	2	7	1	⁴²⁰ˣ3	5	4
²2	⁶⁻1	⁶⁰ˣ4	3	5	²÷6	7
¹²⁺4	7	¹⁷⁺5	6	2	3	⁶⁺1
3	¹⁴⁺5	1	4	²⁵⁺6	7	2
5	6	2	7	4	1	3

203

²÷1	¹⁴⁺3	6	7	¹⁴⁴ˣ2	4	³⁵ˣ5
2	5	¹⁶ˣ4	1	6	3	7
⁸⁺5	¹⁻2	3	4	⁶⁻1	7	³÷6
3	³⁻1	7	5	4	³÷6	2
³⁻7	4	5	⁴⁻6	3	2	²⁻1
4	⁵⁻6	1	2	²⁻7	5	3
¹⁻6	7	³⁰ˣ2	3	5	⁵⁺1	4

204

¹⁵⁺1	4	7	3	³÷6	2	⁵5
¹¹⁺2	7	¹⁵⁺6	4	5	³ˣ3	1
³⁻7	2	²⁴ˣ4	5	¹¹⁺3	1	¹⁻6
4	3	2	6	1	5	7
⁵⁻6	1	³⁰ˣ5	2	²⁸ˣ4	7	3
⁸⁺5	¹²⁺6	3	1	7	²⁻4	²÷2
3	5	1	⁹⁺7	2	6	4

205

18+ 5	7	6	6× 1	2÷ 4	30× 2	3
7+ 3	12+ 4	7	6	2	5	1- 1
4	1	8+ 5	3	1008× 7	6	2
3- 2	5	1· 1	4- 7	3	4	18+ 6
6- 7	11+ 3	2÷ 4	2	6	1	5
1	6	2	1- 4	6+ 5	14+ 3	7
11+ 6	2	3	5	1	7	4

206

120× 6	2	140× 5	7	1	4	16+ 3
4	2÷ 3	6	10× 5	2	1	7
5	3- 4	7	6+ 1	3	2	6
6+ 1	5	2	13+ 3	1- 6	7	8× 4
3	3- 1	4	6	2- 7	5	2
2	20+ 7	120× 3	4	5	14+ 6	1
7	6	1	2	4	3	5

207

16+ 2	3	22+ 7	4× 1	4	1- 5	6
5	4	3	6	1	5- 2	7
6	2	15+ 1	24+ 3	5	17+ 7	2- 4
3÷ 1	7	5	4× 4	3	6	2
3	42+ 1	2	7	6	4	15× 5
7	6	120× 4	5	28× 2	3	1
1- 4	5	6	2	7	1	3· 3

208

10+ 5	3	2	8+ 1	7	24× 4	6
480× 3	2	21+ 4	5	6	49× 7	1
4	1	6	90× 3	5	2	7
588× 2	5	13+ 1	7	3	2÷ 6	4· 4
7	4	5	5- 6	1	3	20+ 2
6	7	11+ 3	4	2	1	5
42× 1	6	7	2	4	5	3

209

⁵⁻7	¹⁴⁺6	1	⁶⁰ˣ5	3	4	²⁺2
2	7	²⁺6	3	⁶⁰ˣ5	1	4
¹⁵⁺3	¹²⁺5	7	²⁻4	6	2	⁶⁻1
4	3	¹⁰ˣ5	2	1	6	7
5	¹²ˣ4	3	²⁺1	2	²³⁺7	6
⁵⁻1	⁴ˣ2	²⁻4	6	7	3	²⁻5
6	1	2	¹⁶⁺7	4	5	3

210

²⁺1	¹⁰ˣ2	5	⁴⁻3	⁷⁺4	¹³⁺6	7
2	5	¹⁸⁺4	²⁴⁰ˣ7	3	¹⁴⁺1	6
²⁻6	7	3	4	5	2	⁸⁺1
4	6	1	5	⁴⁻7	3	2
¹⁰⁵ˣ7	¹⁻3	¹⁴⁺2	6	³⁻1	4	5
5	4	6	²⁺1	⁴⁻2	7	⁴⁻3
3	⁸⁺1	7	2	6	⁹⁺5	4

211

³⁻1	4	⁷⁺2	¹⁻6	7	²⁺3	²⁻5
²⁻5	3	4	1	²⁻2	6	7
³⁶ˣ2	5	7	¹⁷⁺3	4	⁵⁻1	6
3	⁷ˣ1	5	4	¹⁻6	7	²2
6	7	1	5	²⁻3	²⁻2	4
¹⁻7	6	¹¹⁺3	2	5	⁹⁺4	³⁺1
²⁻4	2	6	⁶⁻7	1	5	3

212

³⁰ˣ3	2	¹²⁺6	²¹ˣ1	4	¹⁻5	²⁻7
5	4	2	7	3	⁵⁻1	6
³⁺1	¹⁻5	4	3	²¹⁰ˣ7	²⁸⁸ˣ6	2
2	⁶⁻1	7	5	6	⁴4	3
⁶³⁰ˣ7	3	5	6	1	2	4
¹⁰⁰⁸ˣ6	7	³⁺1	²⁺4	³⁻2	²⁻3	5
4	6	3	2	5	⁸⁺7	1

213

³⁰ˣ 6	³⁻ 4	7	¹⁻ 3	2	¹¹⁺ 1	⁷⁺ 5
1	5	¹²⁺ 6	4	7	3	2
³⁻ 4	1	2	¹⁻ 5	6	⁷⁰ˣ 7	¹²ˣ 3
³ 3	²⁻ 7	5	⁵⁻ 6	1	2	4
³÷ 2	6	⁶⁺ 3	³⁻ 7	4	5	1
¹⁵⁺ 7	3	1	2	¹⁵⁺ 5	4	¹⁻ 6
5	²÷ 2	4	³÷ 1	3	6	7

214

¹⁻ 7	²⁻ 3	¹⁶ˣ 4	¹⁻ 6	5	⁸⁺ 1	¹⁻ 2
6	5	1	4	⁵⁻ 2	7	3
⁷⁺ 1	2	²÷ 6	3	7	³⁻ 5	⁴ 4
¹⁻ 3	4	⁴²ˣ 7	1	6	2	¹⁻ 5
2	¹⁴⁺ 1	5	²⁻ 7	⁹ˣ 3	⁴ 4	6
²⁵⁺ 4	6	2	5	1	3	¹⁴⁺ 7
5	7	3	2	4	6	1

215

⁵⁺ 4	⁴²⁰ˣ 5	2	7	1	3	⁹⁰ˣ 6
1	¹⁸⁺ 4	6	2	³⁻ 5	¹³⁺ 7	3
⁵⁻ 7	3	5	²⁻ 4	2	6	1
2	¹⁶⁺ 7	3	6	²⁰ˣ 4	1	5
¹⁻ 6	2	4	¹ 1	¹⁸⁺ 3	5	¹¹⁺ 7
5	⁷ˣ 1	7	²⁻ 3	6	2	4
²÷ 3	6	1	5	7	²÷ 4	2

216

¹⁶⁺ 4	7	⁶ˣ 1	3	2	²⁴⁰ˣ 6	5
¹²⁺ 6	5	³⁰ˣ 2	³⁻ 7	²÷ 3	4	⁶⁻ 1
5	1	3	4	6	2	7
¹⁶ˣ 2	4	5	⁶⁻ 1	7	¹²⁶ˣ 3	6
⁸⁺ 1	2	¹⁵⁺ 4	6	5	7	¹⁻ 3
7	¹²⁺ 3	⁹⁺ 6	2	1	⁸⁺ 5	4
3	6	¹⁶⁺ 7	5	4	1	2

217

6- 7	4- 5	1	12× 3	4- 6	2	24× 4
1	12+ 3	2	4	210× 5	7	6
2- 3	7	576× 4	1	2	6	2- 5
5	2- 2	3	6	4	3÷ 1	7
9+ 6	4	1- 5	70× 7	6- 1	3	9+ 2
2	1	6	5	7	4	3
17+ 4	6	7	2	9+ 3	5	1

218

1260× 6	5	13+ 2	3	6- 1	7	11+ 4
7	6	3	3- 2	5	4	1
120× 1	3	5	504× 6	4	2	42× 7
5	24× 1	6	4	7	3	2
4	2	3- 7	9+ 1	6	150× 5	3
6× 3	3- 7	4	5 5	2	1	6
2	4	8+ 1	7	2÷ 3	6	5

219

4- 1	5	19+ 6	2	9× 3	4	3- 7
3- 5	4	7	18+ 6	1	3	3÷ 2
2	3÷ 1	3	4	5	6- 7	6
168× 4	3	15+ 2	7	6	1	10+ 5
7	6	5+ 1	5 5	84× 4	2	3
3- 6	9+ 2	4	3	7	1- 5	3- 1
3	7	10× 5	1	2	6	4

220

560× 4	5	14+ 6	2	1- 7	1	3
7	4	1	5	6	3	20+ 2
36× 6	16+ 1	7	3	2÷ 2	4	5
2	3	10× 5	1	12× 4	6	7
2- 5	3÷ 6	2	4	3	12+ 7	7+ 1
3	2	12+ 4	7	1	5	6
6- 1	7	14+ 3	6	5	2÷ 2	4

221

⁴⁰ˣ **4**	⁶⁺ **1**	**5**	⁴⁻ **7**	**2**	**3**	⁴⁸ˣ **6**
5	**7**	⁶ˣ **1**	**3**	¹⁻ **6**	**2**	**4**
¹²ˣ **3**	**4**	**6**	**1**	**7**	³⁻ **5**	**2**
²⁸ˣ **7**	**2**	⁴⁻ **3**	²⁰ˣ **4**	⁶⁺ **5**	¹⁸ˣ **6**	**1**
2	⁹⁰ˣ **6**	**7**	**5**	**1**	⁵⁺ **4**	**3**
⁷⁺ **6**	**5**	²÷ **4**	⁴⁻ **2**	¹⁻ **3**	**1**	²⁻ **7**
1	**3**	**2**	**6**	**4**	⁷ **7**	**5**

222

⁶⁻ **1**	**7**	¹⁰⁰ˣ **5**	**4**	¹¹⁺ **3**	**6**	**2**
²÷ **3**	¹ **1**	²⁰⁺ **4**	**5**	**2**	³¹⁵ˣ **7**	⁵⁻ **6**
6	¹³⁺ **4**	**2**	**7**	**5**	**3**	**1**
7	**2**	⁶ **6**	³⁻ **1**	**4**	**5**	**3**
¹²⁺ **5**	⁷⁺ **6**	**1**	¹²⁺ **3**	**7**	**2**	¹⁵⁺ **4**
2	**5**	³⁶ˣ **3**	**6**	**1**	**4**	**7**
¹⁴⁺ **4**	**3**	**7**	**2**	¹²⁺ **6**	**1**	**5**

223

²÷ **6**	¹⁶ˣ **1**	**4**	¹⁻ **3**	¹³⁺ **7**	**5**	⁹⁺ **2**
3	**4**	²÷ **6**	**2**	¹⁶⁺ **5**	**1**	**7**
¹⁻ **1**	**2**	**3**	**5**	**6**	³⁻ **7**	**4**
¹⁻ **2**	**3**	¹¹⁺ **7**	**4**	¹ **1**	¹⁻ **6**	**5**
³⁵ˣ **7**	¹⁻ **6**	²⁰ˣ **5**	**1**	**4**	²÷ **2**	³÷ **3**
5	**7**	¹¹⁺ **2**	**6**	**3**	**4**	**1**
²⁰ˣ **4**	**5**	**1**	⁷ **7**	¹¹⁺ **2**	**3**	**6**

224

⁶⁰ˣ **6**	¹⁻ **4**	²÷ **2**	**1**	¹⁵⁺ **3**	**7**	**5**
2	**5**	¹³⁺ **3**	**6**	**4**	⁶⁻ **1**	**7**
5	¹⁻ **7**	**6**	²⁶⁺ **4**	**2**	³⁶ˣ **3**	⁸⁺ **1**
³ **3**	⁸⁺ **2**	⁴⁻ **1**	**5**	**7**	**6**	**4**
²⁸ˣ **4**	**1**	**5**	**7**	**6**	**2**	**3**
7	²÷ **3**	²÷ **4**	**2**	¹²⁺ **1**	**5**	**6**
1	**6**	¹⁰⁺ **7**	**3**	⁴⁰ˣ **5**	**4**	**2**

225

5+ **1**	5 **5**	18+ **2**	13+ **7**	**6**	3÷ **3**	1− **4**
4	4× **2**	**6**	4− **3**	**7**	**1**	**5**
2	**1**	**4**	30× **6**	**5**	14+ **7**	16+ **3**
21× **7**	**3**	**1**	2÷ **2**	**4**	**5**	**6**
16+ **3**	**6**	**5**	3− **4**	**1**	**2**	**7**
1− **6**	**7**	84× **3**	3− **5**	**2**	72× **4**	2÷ **1**
5	**4**	**7**	1 **1**	**3**	**6**	**2**

226

6− **7**	**1**	36× **6**	**3**	**2**	1− **5**	**4**
3− **3**	**6**	17+ **1**	**4**	**7**	10× **2**	**5**
1− **5**	**4**	**2**	6× **6**	**3**	8+ **7**	**1**
6× **6**	1− **2**	**3**	**1**	1− **5**	**4**	5− **7**
1	15× **5**	980× **4**	**7**	2− **6**	2− **3**	**2**
2− **2**	**3**	**7**	**5**	**4**	**1**	2÷ **6**
4	35× **7**	**5**	12× **2**	**1**	**6**	**3**

227

4− **7**	**3**	12+ **5**	**1**	**6**	2÷ **4**	**2**
11+ **5**	**4**	14+ **6**	5− **2**	17+ **7**	3× **1**	**3**
2	**5**	**3**	**7**	**4**	**6**	**1**
12× **6**	**2**	168× **7**	**4**	**1**	60× **3**	**5**
1	6− **7**	**2**	6 **6**	**3**	12+ **5**	**4**
1− **3**	**1**	16+ **4**	**5**	12+ **2**	**7**	1− **6**
4	**6**	**1**	**3**	**5**	**2**	**7**

228

24× **4**	84× **6**	**7**	3− **5**	**2**	24× **1**	11+ **3**
6	**7**	20+ **2**	**3**	8+ **5**	**4**	**1**
3	**5**	3÷ **1**	6720× **2**	**4**	**6**	**7**
5	2 **2**	**3**	**4**	42× **1**	**7**	**6**
8+ **1**	**4**	**5**	**6**	**7**	14+ **3**	7+ **2**
5− **7**	**3**	24× **4**	6× **1**	**6**	**2**	**5**
2	**1**	**6**	4− **7**	**3**	**5**	**4**

229

3⁴⁻	**7**	**6**²⁷⁺	**4**	**5**	**1**²ˣ	**2**
2³÷	**6**	**4**¹⁻	**3**	**7**	**5**	**1**
5²⁸⁺	**3**	**1**	**6**⁶⁰ˣ	**4**⁵⁶ˣ	**2**	**7**
7	**1**²÷	**2**	**5**	**3**³	**6**²⁻	**4**
1	**4**	**7**	**2**	**6**⁹⁰ˣ	**3**	**5**
6⁶	**2**¹¹⁺	**5**²⁻	**7**	**1**⁵⁺	**4**	**3**¹²⁶ˣ
4	**5**	**3**⁶⁺	**1**	**2**	**7**	**6**

230

1²÷	**2**	**6**¹²⁶ˣ	**5**	**3**¹⁰⁺	**4**¹⁶⁸ˣ	**7**
7¹⁴⁰ˣ	**4**	**1**	**2**	**5**³⁻	**6**	**3**²÷
4¹⁸⁺	**5**	**3**	**7**	**2**	**1**¹⁴ˣ	**6**
5	**3**	**7**⁷	**6**¹⁸⁺	**1**	**2**	**4**¹¹⁺
6	**1**⁹⁺	**5**	**3**	**4**	**7**	**2**
2³÷	**6**	**4**²÷	**1**¹¹⁺	**7**	**3**⁹⁺	**5**
3⁴⁻	**7**	**2**	**4**	**6**	**5**	**1**

231

3²⁻	**2**³⁶ˣ	**4**¹⁵⁺	**7**	**1**⁶ˣ	**6**	**5**¹⁻
5	**1**	**3**	**4**	**2**⁹⁺	**7**	**6**
7¹⁶⁸⁰ˣ	**5**	**6**	**3**⁹⁺	**4**⁷²ˣ	**2**²÷	**1**
2	**7**⁶⁻	**1**	**5**	**6**	**4**¹²ˣ	**3**
4	**6**	**2**²	**1**	**3**	**5**³⁵ˣ	**7**
1⁵⁻	**4**¹⁴⁺	**7**	**6**⁶⁰ˣ	**5**²⁻	**3**	**2**²÷
6	**3**	**5**	**2**	**7**⁸⁺	**1**	**4**

232

2²÷	**5**²⁰ˣ	**7**⁵⁻	**1**¹⁶⁺	**4**⁴	**6**¹⁷⁺	**3**
1	**4**	**2**	**3**	**5**	**7**	**6**
5²⁻	**3**	**6**¹⁴⁺	**4**⁵⁶ˣ	**7**⁶⁻	**1**	**2**
6³÷	**2**	**3**	**7**	**1**³⁻	**4**	**5**⁹⁺
7⁶⁻	**1**	**5**	**2**	**6**²÷	**3**	**4**
3¹⁻	**7**¹⁻	**4**³⁻	**6**³⁰⁰ˣ	**2**	**5**	**1**⁴²ˣ
4	**6**	**1**	**5**	**3**	**2**	**7**

233

35× 5	6− 7	10+ 4	3	1− 2	1	60× 6
7	1	3	168× 4	6	2	5
12+ 2	4	210× 5	7	2÷ 3	6	12× 1
6	3 3	7	13+ 2	4− 1	5	4
2÷ 1	2	6	5	3− 4	7	3
1− 3	30× 6	9+ 2	1	5	13+ 4	7
4	5	1	6	10+ 7	3	2

234

17+ 6	3× 1	3	2− 5	18+ 4	2	7
7	2	1	3	5	72× 6	4
2	245× 7	5	2− 6	8× 1	4	3
17+ 3	2÷ 6	7	4	2	8+ 1	4− 5
5	3	48× 4	2	6	7	1
4	5	42× 6	1	7	1− 3	2
3− 1	4	42× 2	7	3	1− 5	6

235

120× 5	4	2− 1	3	8+ 2	28× 7	1− 6
6	16+ 3	2	1	5	4	7
6× 3	5	6	210× 7	28× 1	2÷ 2	4
1	2− 6	4	5	7	1− 3	2
2	6− 1	10+ 7	6	4	2− 5	3
13+ 4	7	3	36× 2	6	5− 1	4− 5
7	2	1− 5	4	3	6	1

236

84× 2	6− 7	2÷ 6	3	120× 5	4	10× 1
7	1	240× 3	4	6	9+ 2	5
6	36× 3	28× 1	5	4	7	2
5 5	6	4	5− 7	2	18× 1	3
8+ 4	2	7	12+ 1	3	2− 5	6
1	9+ 5	2	6	14+ 7	3	3− 4
3	4	3− 5	2	1	6	7

237

⁴⁻ 1	¹⁸⁺ 7	6	5	¹⁻ 4	3	²÷ 2
5	⁸⁴⁰ˣ 3	7	⁴ˣ 1	2	²⁰⁺ 6	4
²¹ˣ 3	5	4	2	7	1	¹²⁰ˣ 6
7	1	2	³ 3	6	4	5
²÷ 4	¹⁻ 2	3	²⁻ 6	²⁻ 5	7	⁶⁻ 1
2	⁵⁻ 6	1	4	²⁻ 3	5	7
²⁻ 6	4	¹³⁺ 5	7	1	¹⁻ 2	3

238

⁴⁻ 7	3	⁴⁰ˣ 5	⁶⁻ 1	¹⁰⁺ 6	4	²÷ 2
¹⁴⁺ 5	4	2	7	3	1	¹⁶⁸ˣ 6
4	³⁺ 2	1	²÷ 6	²⁻ 5	3	7
2	²⁵ˣ 5	7	3	⁵⁻ 1	6	4
3	7	6	²⁰⁺ 4	³⁻ 2	5	1
¹³⁺ 6	¹ 1	4	5	7	²¹⁰ˣ 2	3
1	6	⁹⁺ 3	2	4	7	5

239

³⁻ 2	¹⁻ 3	⁹⁺ 1	4	¹⁻ 5	²¹ˣ 7	⁷⁻ 6
5	2	4	⁵⁻ 7	6	3	1
³⁶ˣ 6	⁷⁺ 4	3	2	⁶⁻ 7	1	³⁰ˣ 5
1	6	¹⁶⁺ 7	5	4	2	3
⁶⁻ 7	1	³⁰ˣ 6	³÷ 3	¹⁻ 2	¹⁻ 5	4
³⁻ 4	7	5	1	3	⁴⁻ 6	2
²⁻ 3	5	⁹⁺ 2	6	1	³⁻ 4	7

240

⁴²ˣ 2	3	⁸ˣ 1	¹⁰⁺ 6	4	¹⁷⁺ 5	7
7	¹³⁺ 4	2	³÷ 1	3	¹⁴⁺ 6	5
3	6	4	²¹ˣ 2	⁴⁻ 5	7	1
²÷ 4	2	7	5	1	²÷ 3	6
²⁵ˣ 5	1	¹⁴⁺ 6	7	⁵⁶ˣ 2	⁸⁺ 4	3
¹⁴⁺ 6	5	3	4	7	1	⁸⁺ 2
1	7	5	³⁻ 3	6	2	4

241

18× 1	6	9+ 2	84× 4	3	7	2− 5
140× 4	3	1	6	7+ 2	5	7
5	7	120× 4	105× 3	28× 1	3÷ 2	6
6	2	5	7	4	3÷ 1	3
6× 2	1	3	5	7	2− 6	4
3	16+ 5	84× 7	2	2− 6	4	2÷ 1
7	4	6	9+ 1	5	3	2

242

5+ 1	4	84× 7	2	6	2− 3	5
19+ 4	6	3	2− 5	4− 1	14× 7	2
2	42× 3	4	7	5	120× 6	1
7	2	10+ 6	1	3	5	4
2− 5	7	12+ 2	3	4	5− 1	6
2÷ 3	4− 5	1	6	2	2÷ 4	4− 7
6	1	140× 5	4	7	2	3

243

4− 3	2÷ 1	2	30× 5	1− 6	7	1− 4
7	16+ 6	1	2	3	80× 4	5
3÷ 6	7	3	3÷ 1	4	5	2÷ 2
2	11+ 4	7	3	1− 5	6	1
7+ 1	2	140× 5	4	7	12+ 3	6
4	13+ 5	15+ 6	7	2	14× 1	3
5	3	11+ 4	6	1	2	7

244

7+ 1	3	2	360× 4	1470× 7	5	6
2÷ 4	1	3	6	5	2	7
2	140× 4	1	5	1− 6	7	3
3− 5	2	16+ 4	7	3	5− 6	1
2− 7	5	6	1	2	1− 3	4
2÷ 3	6	2− 7	2	5+ 4	4− 1	5
1− 6	7	5	3	1	2÷ 4	2

245

3÷1	3	1−2	16+5	3−7	2−6	4
3−2	5	3	6	4	49×1	7
24+6	1	56×4	2	3	7	90×5
4	2	7	1	30×5	3	6
7	6	1·1	14+4	2	8+5	3
12×3	4	11+5	7	6×6	2	1
2−5	7	6	3	1	2÷4	2

246

35×7	5	19+4	1	6	6×3	2
9+1	3	6	4·4	2	16+5	7
5	16+6	11+1	3	7	12+2	4
3	7	12×2	2−5	4−1	4	6
2÷4	2	3	7	5	14+6	15×1
2	5+4	16+7	6	3	1	5
6·6	1	40×5	2	4	7	3

247

12+6	2	14+4	5·5	7×1	210×3	7
3	4	6	2÷2	7	1	5
1	3	7	4	1−6	5	2
1−4	5	6+1	3	2	1−7	6
2÷2	1	2100×3	7	5	2−6	4
210×7	6	5	6×1	4	6×2	3
5	9+7	2	6	1−3	4	1

248

13+7	2÷2	4	30×6	1	5	14+3
5	3÷3	1	5−7	2÷4	2	6
1	1−4	21×3	2	36×6	1−7	5
13+4	5	7	3	2	6	10+1
6	5−1	21+5	4	7	12×3	2
3	6	2÷2	1	5	4	7
5−2	7	90×6	5	3	5+1	4

249

¹⁷⁺5	^{48×}2	4	^{3÷}1	3	¹⁴⁺7	6
3	6	^{2−}5	7	^{1−}4	1	¹²⁺2
7	^{3÷}1	3	^{30×}2	5	6	4
2	¹¹⁺4	7	5	^{2÷}6	3	¹1
¹¹⁺4	^{1−}7	6	3	^{6−}1	¹⁰⁺2	5
1	^{2−}5	^{3÷}2	6	7	¹⁶⁺4	3
6	3	^{8×}1	4	2	5	7

250

^{1−}4	3	^{4−}7	⁸⁺1	^{1−}5	6	¹¹⁺2
^{5−}2	^{48×}6	3	7	¹⁵⁺1	5	4
7	2	4	3	6	¹²⁺1	5
^{4−}3	7	^{25×}1	5	⁴4	2	6
⁷⁺6	⁹⁺4	5	¹¹⁺2	7	3	¹¹⁺1
1	5	^{3÷}6	^{2−}4	2	⁷7	3
^{4−}5	1	2	6	^{1−}3	4	7

251

^{3−}5	¹¹⁺1	4	^{147×}7	3	^{3÷}2	6
2	6	^{3−}1	4	7	³3	¹⁸⁺5
^{1−}3	2	¹⁸⁺6	^{3−}1	4	¹⁰⁺5	7
^{3−}4	7	5	^{3−}3	6	1	2
^{1−}6	5	7	^{1−}2	1	4	3
^{6−}7	⁹⁺4	^{15×}3	5	¹⁹⁺2	6	1
1	3	2	6	5	^{3−}7	4

252

¹⁵⁺5	^{144×}3	2	4	¹⁴⁺6	7	1
1	7	^{12×}4	6	^{2−}3	5	^{40×}2
^{126×}6	2	3	^{6−}7	1	4	5
7	⁵⁺1	⁵5	^{2÷}2	4	^{3−}6	3
3	4	^{6−}1	^{2−}5	7	^{48×}2	6
¹²⁺2	6	7	¹⁵⁺3	⁶⁺5	1	4
4	5	6	1	^{42×}2	3	7

253

5 ¹⁻	4	2 ⁴⁻	1	6	7 ⁴⁻	3
1 ⁶ˣ	6	3	5	7	2 ²÷	4
4 ¹⁴⁺	5 ¹⁸⁺	6	7	2	3 ¹⁻	1 ¹²ˣ
3	7	5 ¹⁰⁺	4	1	6	2
7 ⁴²ˣ	2 ²÷	4 ⁴	3 ⁸⁺	5	1 ⁵⁺	6 ¹⁻
6	1	7 ¹²⁺	2	3	4	5
2 ⁵⁺	3	1 ¹¹⁺	6	4	5 ¹²⁺	7

254

7 ⁶⁻	1	5	6	3 ²⁵²ˣ	4	2 ²÷
1 ⁴⁻	5	6	7	2	3 ¹¹⁺	4
4 ⁴	6 ¹²ˣ	2	3 ⁶⁰ˣ	5 ⁴⁹⁰ˣ	7	1
6 ¹¹⁺	2	1	4	7	5 ⁵	3
3	7 ³⁻	4	5	1	2	6 ¹⁸⁰ˣ
2 ¹⁻	3	7 ²⁶⁺	1	4	6	5
5 ⁹⁺	4	3 ⁵⁺	2	6	1	7

255

1 ⁶ˣ	7 ¹⁸⁺	3	2	4	6 ³⁶⁰ˣ	5
6	1	2	5 ²⁻	7 ⁴⁻	3	4
4 ²⁰ˣ	2 ²÷	1	7	3	5 ⁴⁰ˣ	6 ¹¹⁺
3	6	7 ⁸⁺	1	5 ⁵	4	2
7	5 ³⁰ˣ	6	4 ¹⁹⁺	2	1	3
5 ³⁰ˣ	3	4 ¹³⁺	6	1	2 ⁹⁸ˣ	7
2	4	5	3	6	7	1

256

4 ⁵⁸⁸⁰ˣ	6 ⁴²ˣ	1	7	3 ¹⁻	2	5 ⁹⁺
6	7	2 ²÷	4	5	1	3
7	5	4	1 ²÷	2	3 ²¹⁺	6
2 ¹³⁺	4	7	3 ³	6 ¹⁻	5	1
5 ¹⁰ˣ	2	3 ²⁻	6 ⁵⁻	1	4	7
3 ³ˣ	1	5	2 ¹⁴⁺	7	6 ⁴⁸ˣ	4
1	3 ²÷	6	5	4 ¹¹⁺	7	2

257

120×2	5	6+1	35×7	3−3	6	10+4
3	4	2	5	1008×7	12+1	6
13+5	17+2	3	4	6	7	1
1	7	5	6	2÷4	2	3
7	3	168×6	1	4−5	9+4	2
17+4	6	7	1−2	1	3	2−5
6	1	4	3	7+2	5	7

258

252×7	3	15+6	10+4	5	1	6+2
4	7	2	1−6	2÷1	1−5	3
3	48×4	9+5	7	2	6	1
3−5	2	3	6−1	7	2−4	6
2	6	1	3−5	2÷3	4−7	140×4
15+1	1−5	4	2	6	3	7
6	1	7	24×3	4	2	5

259

1−6	120×4	15+7	2	5	9+3	3÷1
7	5	6	1	2	4	3
11+5	6	12×4	3	1	5−2	7
30×3	2	5	2−7	11+4	1	6
5−2	7	6×1	5	630×3	2−6	4
8+1	3	2	2−4	6	14+7	5
4	1	3	6	7	5	2

260

72×6	2−7	5	17+3	2	5−1	2÷4
3	5−1	5+4	7	5	6	2
4	6	1	8+2	2−3	5	22+7
24×2	4	3	1	6	7	5
13+1	5+2	1−6	5	3−7	4	3
5	3	7	3−4	1	1−2	5−6
7	3−5	2	2−6	4	3	1

261

²¹⁰ˣ5	1	¹⁸⁺6	⁶⁺3	⁵⁶⁰ˣ4	7	⁵⁻2
6	4	2	1	7	5	²⁻3
7	6	²³⁺1	2	3	4	5
⁸⁴ˣ3	2	4	6	5	¹⁷⁺1	7
2	7	²⁻5	4	⁵⁻1	3	6
¹²ˣ1	3	7	³⁵ˣ5	6	²÷2	4
4	²⁻5	3	7	³÷2	6	¹1

262

⁵⁻6	1	¹⁶⁸ˣ7	¹⁻4	⁶⁺2	¹⁵ˣ5	3
²÷2	4	6	5	3	1	³⁻7
1	⁴²ˣ2	¹⁰⁵ˣ3	7	5	¹³⁺6	4
3	7	¹¹⁺4	6	1	2	5
²⁻5	⁷⁺6	1	¹⁻3	³⁻4	7	²÷2
7	³⁰ˣ3	5	2	¹⁷⁺6	4	1
⁹⁺4	5	2	1	7	²÷3	6

263

²⁴ˣ4	¹⁶⁺3	6	⁴⁻1	5	⁵⁻7	2
3	³÷2	1	6	¹⁶⁺7	4	5
2	6	²÷4	¹⁵⁺5	¹³⁺3	⁸⁺1	²⁸ˣ7
⁸⁺7	1	2	3	6	5	4
¹²⁺1	²⁻5	⁶⁰ˣ3	7	4	2	⁶6
6	7	5	4	⁶⁺2	3	1
5	¹⁴⁺4	7	2	1	²÷6	3

264

⁴²ˣ6	7	¹⁴⁺1	¹²⁺2	⁸⁺5	¹⁻4	3
⁴⁸ˣ4	6	7	3	2	1	¹⁰ˣ5
3	4	5	³⁻7	²÷6	2	1
¹³⁺7	1	2	¹²⁺6	3	⁵5	³⁻4
5	³÷2	6	1	¹⁻4	3	7
²÷1	¹⁻3	4	5	7	¹⁻6	³÷2
2	⁸⁺5	3	⁴4	⁸⁺1	7	6

265

2−5	36×2	3	5−6	1	8×4	3−7
3	6	17+7	5	2	1	4
12×1	8+4	5	13+7	315×3	3÷2	6
6	3	2	4	5	6−7	1
2	1	8×4	3	7	1−6	5
3−4	210×7	1	2	14+6	5	1−3
7	5	6	3−1	4	3	2

266

2÷6	3	20×4	5	2−2	14+7	1
14+1	6	21×3	7	4	7+5	2
7	420×5	6	18×1	3	2	4
11+4	7	2	6	1	2−3	5
20×2	1	7	2−3	5	2−4	16+6
5	2	1	17+4	7	6	3
1−3	4	10×5	2	6	1 1	7

267

84×3	4	18+5	7	1	2−2	420×6
1	7	2÷3	6	5	4	2
120×4	12×6	10+1	90×2	3	5	7
6	2	7	5	8+4	1	3
5	1	2	3	6 6	17+7	4
10+7	3	3−4	1	19+2	2÷6	5
3−2	5	6	4	7	3	1

268

144×6	2	12+3	5	4	2÷1	6−7
3	4	35×5	7	15+6	2	1
30×5	3	336×2	1	7	4	6
1	5 5	4	6	2	4−7	3
2	1	7	8+3	14+5	6	11+4
24+7	6	1	4	3	2−5	2
4	7	9+6	2	1	3	5

269

3 [1−]	4	1 [35×]	5	7	6 [3÷]	2
5 [6+]	2 [5−]	7	4 [1−]	3	1 [5−]	6
1	3 [30×]	5	2	6 [26+]	7	4 [8+]
7 [2−]	5	2 [3÷]	6	4	3 [3]	1
2 [2−]	1 [42×]	6	7	5	4	3
4	6 [3−]	3	1 [1−]	2	5 [2−]	7
6 [1−]	7	4 [12×]	3	1	2 [7+]	5

270

1 [72×]	6	2	5 [12+]	3	4	7 [28×]
6	3 [4−]	5 [2−]	7	4 [2÷]	2	1
2 [42×]	7	1 [19+]	6	5 [2−]	3	4
3	4 [11+]	7	2	6 [6]	1 [4−]	5
7	2 [2÷]	6	4	1 [4−]	5	3 [11+]
5 [17+]	1	3 [1−]	2	7	6	2
4	5	3	1 [14+]	7	6	2

271

1 [30×]	6	3 [14+]	4	7	2 [9+]	5
5	4 [13+]	1 [10+]	6	3	7 [18+]	2
4 [140×]	2	7	3 [2−]	6	5	1 [1]
7	5	4 [2÷]	1	2 [10×]	6 [2÷]	3
6 [126×]	7	2	5	1	3 [84×]	4
3	1 [210×]	6 [60×]	2	5	4 [96×]	7
2	3	5	7	4	1	6

272

6 [5−]	7 [6−]	1	4 [60×]	5	3	2 [1−]
1	6 [13+]	4 [56×]	7	2	5 [16+]	3
5	2	6 [17+]	1	3	4	7
3 [9+]	4	2	5	1	7 [210×]	6
2	3 [60×]	7 [1−]	6	4 [17+]	1 [8+]	5
4	5	3 [8+]	2 [1−]	7	6	1
7 [8+]	1	5	3	6	2 [2÷]	4

273

1- 4	168× 7	1- 3	2	5 5	5- 1	6
3	4	6	9+ 7	2	450× 5	1
5- 6	1	1- 5	4	21+ 7	3	2
13+ 7	2÷ 2	1	3 3	6	4	5
1	5	1- 7	6	4	15+ 2	3
3- 2	13+ 3	4	4- 5	1	6	7
5	6	2÷ 2	1	84× 3	7	4

274

5+ 1	300× 2	5	6	504× 3	336× 4	7
4	5	1	3	7	6	2
1- 6	7	2	1	4	42× 3	12+ 5
3÷ 3	1	10+ 6	3- 2	5	7	4
1- 5	6	4	12+ 7	9+ 1	2	3
5- 7	18+ 4	3	5	2	30× 1	6
2	3 3	7	4	6	5	1

275

60× 5	1	5+ 2	3- 7	3- 4	3- 3	6
6	2- 5	3	4	1	3- 7	3- 2
2	7	22+ 1	6	3	4	5
21× 3	2÷ 6	7	2 2	5	2÷ 1	3- 4
7	3	15+ 4	5	6	2	1
3- 1	4	1- 5	3÷ 3	9+ 2	42× 6	7
2÷ 4	2	6	1	7	2- 5	3

276

30× 6	1	5	16+ 7	3	4	2
35× 7	5	6× 6	2- 4	4- 1	180× 2	3
2÷ 4	4- 7	1	2	5	3÷ 3	6
2	3	17+ 7	6	4	1	5
14+ 5	4	2	3	42× 6	7	1
2÷ 1	2	105× 3	5	7	2- 6	4
13+ 3	6	4	1	14+ 2	5	7

277

3− 4	3− 2	35× 5	7	6	12+ 3	14× 1
7	5	10+ 6	4	3	6× 1	2
4− 5	1	9+ 2	1− 3	4	6	7
2÷ 2	4	3	7+ 6	1	2− 7	5
3÷ 1	3	4	2− 5	7	3− 2	13+ 6
3− 3	1− 6	6− 7	1	11+ 2	5	4
6	7	2÷ 1	2	5	4	3

278

24× 2	7	6	1− 4	5	3÷ 3	1
4	3	10+ 2	7	1− 1	6	12+ 5
105× 7	5	3	6	19+ 2	1	2− 4
3	5− 2	7	5+ 1	4	5	6
5	30× 6	1	1− 3	7	4	2 2
11+ 1	4	5	2	126× 6	7	3
6	5+ 1	4	2− 5	3	5− 2	7

279

1− 4	126× 2	3	7	12+ 1	5	13+ 6
5	3	7+ 2	1	4	6	7
13+ 6	4	12+ 7	2	3	20× 1	5
3	4− 5	1	2÷ 6	5− 2	7	4
14× 7	2− 6	4	3	7+ 5	2	1 1
1	14+ 7	15+ 5	4	6	420× 3	1− 2
2	1	6	5	7	4	3

280

5− 2	3÷ 1	2− 7	20× 4	5	2÷ 6	3
7	3	5	4− 1	17+ 4	2	6
18+ 6	5+ 2	3	5	13+ 7	4	1
5	6	1− 4	3	2	1	7 7
1	10+ 4	6	9+ 2	3	16+ 7	3− 5
1− 4	2− 5	2÷ 1	7	6	3	2
3	7	2	5− 6	1	1− 5	4

281

^{840×}7	2	5	¹⁰⁺1	3	¹⁰⁺4	6
4	3	³¹⁺7	6	²2	^{60×}5	^{2−}1
¹³⁺5	4	6	¹²⁺7	1	2	3
3	5	4	2	6	^{6−}1	7
²2	7	1	3	^{72×}4	6	^{1−}5
⁸⁺6	1	2	^{700×}5	7	3	4
1	^{2÷}6	3	4	5	^{5−}7	2

282

^{24×}4	3	^{2−}5	1	6	^{5−}2	7
2	¹⁵⁺5	7	⁵⁺4	1	^{2÷}6	3
3	2	^{2−}4	6	^{2−}5	7	⁸⁺1
5	⁴4	^{1−}6	7	^{3÷}3	1	2
^{42×}1	6	^{6×}2	3	7	^{3−}4	5
^{42×}6	7	^{2−}1	^{3−}5	2	3	4
7	1	3	^{2−}2	4	^{1−}5	6

283

^{2÷}2	4	^{60×}5	^{42×}3	6	1	7
^{3−}6	3	4	2	5	7	⁶⁺1
3	¹¹⁺6	2	7	^{8×}1	4	5
^{4−}5	²³⁺7	3	1	2	²¹⁺6	4
1	2	7	4	3	5	6
¹⁸⁺4	5	1	^{720×}6	^{84×}7	2	3
7	1	6	5	4	³3	2

284

^{3−}4	^{15×}1	3	^{4−}6	2	⁹⁺5	⁹⁺7
7	5	¹⁶⁺6	1	¹⁵⁺3	4	2
^{180×}3	4	7	2	1	^{12×}6	¹⁵⁺5
5	3	¹1	7	4	2	6
¹⁵⁺2	6	^{120×}5	3	^{35×}7	1	4
6	¹³⁺7	2	4	5	^{4−}3	^{3÷}1
1	2	4	^{1−}5	6	7	3

285

1680× 5	7	4	2÷ 1	2	2÷ 6	3
4	1	3	5− 2	7	5	6
60× 2	1− 4	5	126× 6	11+ 1	3	7
6	5	10+ 2	3	28× 4	7	1
1	2	6	7	60× 3	4	5
13+ 3	14+ 6	7	1− 4	5	2÷ 1	2
7	3	1	1− 5	6	2÷ 2	4

286

90× 5	6	3	2÷ 1	22+ 4	5− 7	2
13+ 7	1	1− 6	2	3	5	4
3	4 4	7	12+ 5	1− 2	1	6
2	17+ 7	5	4	1 1	3− 6	3
9+ 6	5	2÷ 2	3	3− 7	4	11+ 1
1	2	4	1− 6	1− 5	3	7
12× 4	3	1	7	6	3− 2	5

287

1− 6	15× 5	15× 2	3− 4	7	2− 3	1
5	3	6	7	1− 2	3− 1	4
6× 3	10+ 2	5	6	1	3− 4	7
1	7	15× 3	5	2− 4	6	2 2
2	1	1− 4	3	2÷ 6	2− 7	5
3− 7	24× 4	10+ 1	2	3	1− 5	6
4	6	7	4− 1	5	1− 2	3

288

60× 5	2	12+ 7	4	1	14+ 6	10+ 3
6	12+ 3	2÷ 4	2	7	1	5
6+ 1	4	5	14+ 6	60× 3	7 7	2
2	3÷ 1	3	7	5	2− 4	6
3	1− 5	6	1	4	5− 2	7
1176× 7	6	3÷ 1	3	10+ 2	5	3− 4
4	7	60× 2	5	6	3	1

289

48× 6	4− 3	7	3÷ 1	7+ 2	5	140× 4
2	2− 4	6	3	1	7	5
4	10+ 1	2	7	14+ 5	1008× 3	6
2− 3	5	2− 4	2	6	1 1	7
35× 7	30× 6	1	5	3	4	2
1	2− 7	5	2− 6	2÷ 4	2	2− 3
5	1− 2	3	4	1− 7	6	1

290

1− 4	5	36× 6	3	2	6− 1	7
10+ 5	3	2	15+ 4	42× 7	6	1
12+ 2	1	3	7	1− 5	4	60× 6
3	3− 7	4	6× 1	3÷ 6	2	5
7	12+ 4	5 5	6	10+ 1	14+ 3	2
6	2	1	5	3	7	4
14+ 1	6	7	2÷ 2	4	2− 5	3

291

588× 7	1	3	15+ 2	360× 4	5	6
4	7	6	5	2	3	1
1− 3	4	420× 7	6+ 1	5	3÷ 6	2
2	6	5	13+ 4	8+ 7	1	3 3
12+ 5	12× 3	4	6	1	2	140× 7
6	60× 2	11+ 1	7	3	17+ 4	5
1	5	2	3	6	7	4

292

3− 4	3− 5	3	1− 2	840× 7	10+ 6	1
1	2	6	4	5	3	1− 7
2− 5	3	11+ 4	19+ 7	2	80× 1	6
6− 7	1	2	3	6 6	5	4
4− 3	7	5	6	1	4	19+ 2
3÷ 6	2− 4	15+ 7	1	3	2	5
2	6	4− 1	5	4	7	3

293

36×			16+	35×		
3	**2**	**6**	**4**	**5**	**7**	**1**
120×					10+	
4	**5**	**3**	**2**	**7**	**1**	**6**
	105×		126×	160×		
6	**1**	**5**	**7**	**2**	**4**	**3**
6−						3−
1	**3**	**7**	**6**	**4**	**5**	**2**
	2÷			9+		
7	**4**	**2**	**3**	**1**	**6**	**5**
20+		72×				14+
5	**6**	**4**	**1**	**3**	**2**	**7**
			5			
2	**7**	**1**	**5**	**6**	**3**	**4**

294

17+	420×				12+	3÷
2	**4**	**7**	**5**	**3**	**1**	**6**
		17+		1−		
5	**1**	**3**	**4**	**7**	**6**	**2**
			17+			
7	**2**	**5**	**3**	**6**	**4**	**1**
6	27×			21×		
6	**5**	**4**	**2**	**1**	**7**	**3**
8+					60×	
3	**7**	**1**	**6**	**2**	**5**	**4**
						14+
1	**6**	**2**	**7**	**4**	**3**	**5**
	90×					
4	**3**	**6**	**1**	**5**	**2**	**7**

295

84×	18+		16+			9+
6	**3**	**7**	**5**	**1**	**4**	**2**
			12+			
2	**7**	**5**	**1**	**6**	**3**	**4**
10+					10+	
1	**4**	**3**	**6**	**5**	**2**	**7**
	4−		14+	56×		
5	**6**	**2**	**3**	**4**	**7**	**1**
3÷					1−	
3	**1**	**4**	**7**	**2**	**5**	**6**
16+		84×			15×	
4	**5**	**6**	**2**	**7**	**1**	**3**
	1−		4	2÷		
7	**2**	**1**	**4**	**3**	**6**	**5**

296

8×	16+			15×		1−
2	**1**	**6**	**4**	**5**	**3**	**7**
	120×		15+			
4	**3**	**5**	**2**	**7**	**1**	**6**
		14+		17+	140×	
1	**2**	**3**	**5**	**6**	**7**	**4**
3						
3	**4**	**7**	**6**	**2**	**5**	**1**
1260×			12+		3÷	
7	**5**	**4**	**1**	**3**	**6**	**2**
		13+			30×	
5	**6**	**1**	**7**	**4**	**2**	**3**
				3−		
6	**7**	**2**	**3**	**1**	**4**	**5**

297

8+ 1	**4−** 5	**84×** 7	3	4	**3÷** 2	**2−** 6
7	1	**10+** 3	2	5	6	4
1− 5	4	**18×** 1	6	3	**5−** 7	2
9+ 4	**3−** 3	6	**2−** 7	**1−** 2	1	**4−** 5
3	**9+** 7	2	5	**2−** 6	4	1
2	**2−** 6	4	**5+** 1	**105×** 7	5	3
13+ 6	2	5	4	**11+** 1	3	7

298

1− 6	7	**120×** 1	5	4	**1−** 3	2
2÷ 4	2	**28+** 7	6	3	**6+** 5	1
4− 1	4	6	7	5	**2÷** 2	**10+** 3
5	3	**12+** 4	2	6	1	7
126× 3	6	**7+** 2	**1−** 4	**2÷** 1	**18+** 7	5
7	**8+** 1	5	3	2	**14+** 4	6
2	5	**3÷** 3	1	**7** 7	6	4

299

4− 5	**3−** 4	1	**42×** 7	2	3	**1−** 6
1	**14+** 7	4	3	**3÷** 6	2	5
210× 7	3	5	**3÷** 2	**96×** 4	6	1
2	**2−** 1	3	6	**2−** 5	7	4
180× 3	2	**24×** 6	4	1	**420×** 5	7
6	5	**10+** 2	1	7	4	3
24× 4	6	**15+** 7	5	3	**2÷** 1	2

300

40× 5	4	**14+** 6	1	3	**42×** 2	7
2	**2−** 7	5	4	**5−** 1	6	3
24× 4	**1−** 6	7	**15×** 3	**2÷** 2	1	**13+** 5
3	2	**2÷** 4	5	**2−** 6	7	1
12+ 1	5	2	**7** 7	4	**25+** 3	**2−** 6
6	**14+** 3	**10+** 1	2	7	5	4
7	1	3	6	5	4	2